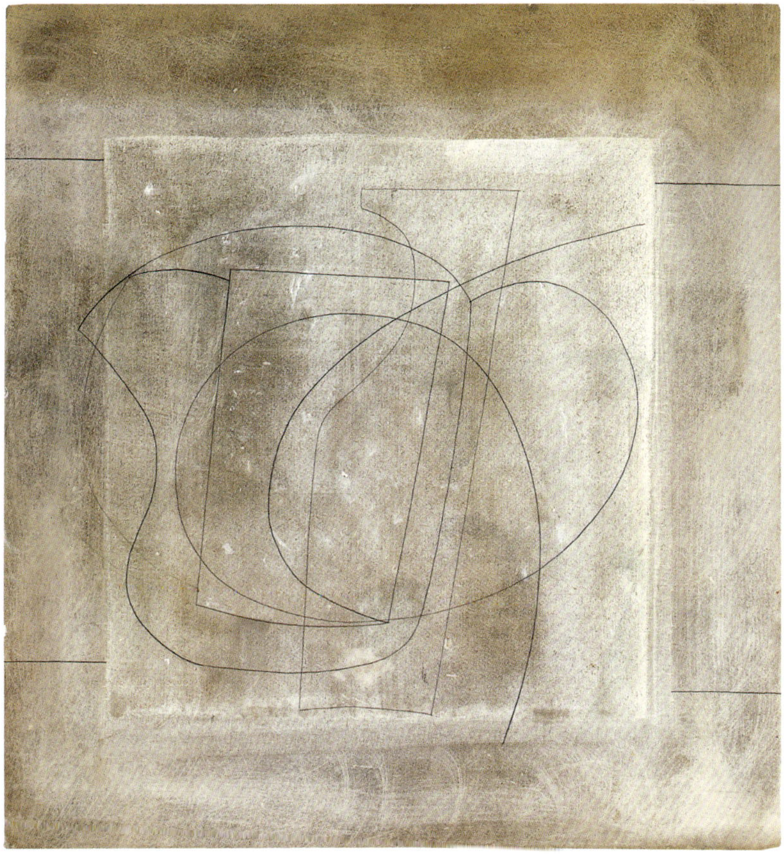

Ben Nicholson

'chasing out something alive'

drawings and painted reliefs 1950-75

ACKNOWLEDGEMENTS

We are grateful to Peter Khoroche for bringing an entirely fresh view to our perception of Nicholson's work. We share with him in thanking the many private owners and curators of public collections, both here and abroad, who have allowed us to make an exhibition of such richness.

Many people have been especially helpful, amongst them Mariuccia Sprenger, Janey McAllester of the Bernard Jacobson Gallery, Sally Lescher of Conservation Management, Dany Ardouin of the Helly Nahmad Gallery, Sophie Oppenheimer, Sarah Thomas of Sotheby's, Madeleine Howell of Christie's, Michelle Archer of Waddington's, Caroline Lelièvre, Rosemary Muir, Catherine Clement and her colleagues at the Tate, Isobel Johnstone, Frances Munk and Jill Constantine at the Hayward Gallery, Caroline Bacon at the Cecil Higgins Art Gallery, Diana Eccles at the British Council, Antony Griffiths and Janice Reading at the British Museum, Frances Guy at Pallant House, Alistair Hicks and Lucille Zacaria at the Deutsche Bank Collection, Janice Slater and Alice Dewey at the Scottish National Gallery of Modern Art, Robert Hall at Huddersfield Art Gallery, Geraldine Glynn at the Ashmolean Museum and Iona Serghiuta of Re:source. Angela Verren Taunt has been extremely supportive throughout the exhibition's preparations.

We are pleased to have collaborated with the organisation Vocaleyes in the preparation of audio and other aids to help visually impaired people to enjoy the exhibition.

The exhibition has been generously supported by The Henry Moore Foundation and the Friends of Kettle's Yard, and Christie's have contributed towards the costs of this catalogue.

CHRISTIE'S

Finally, we are delighted that, after its showing in Cambridge, the exhibition will travel on to the Whitworth Art Gallery in Manchester and Southampton City Art Gallery.

MH

overleaf
1968 (crescent moonlight)
56.5 x 50.8 cm (cat. 38)

PREFACE

It is now almost twenty years since Kettle's Yard presented the exhibition *Ben Nicholson: the years of experiment 1919-39.*

Our new exhibition looks to Nicholson's mature years and brings together the two aspects of his work which he felt to be the most important of the period 1950 to 1975. The reliefs, which he carved and painted, find him at his most abstract and frequently at his most austere and monumental. By contrast, the drawings reveal him at his most intimate, spontaneous and figurative, many of them chronicling the journeys he made through Italy, Greece, France and Portugal, to Yorkshire and East Anglia.

The exhibition has been devised and selected by Peter Khoroche and follows the publication by Lund Humphries of his book, *Ben Nicholson:drawings and painted reliefs.*

Michael Harrison
Director, Kettle's Yard

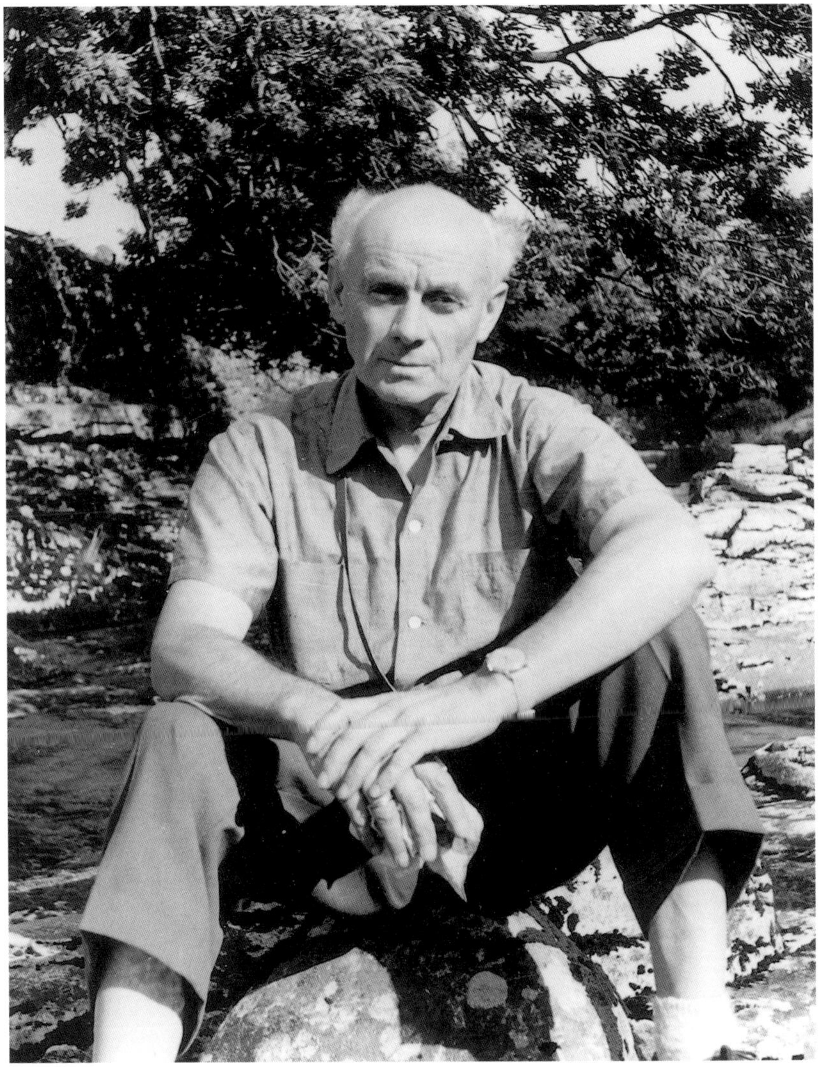

Ben Nicholson at Yockenthwaite, Wharfedale, 1957

‘CHASING OUT SOMETHING *ALIVE*’

Peter Khoroche

1950 – ends and beginnings

In May 1949 William Nicholson, master of illusion, poet of the surface of things, virtuoso handler of paint, died at the age of seventy-seven. It was some years since he had painted his last picture, but now his long career, which had begun in the 1890s – in the world of Kipling and Beerbohm – inexorably became part of history. No one felt the finality of it more than William's son, Ben. Suddenly the living link with his own artistic formation was gone and the complex relationship with his painter-father relegated to the past.

Ever since coming to Cornwall ten years before, he had been working in cramped quarters at home. But later in that same year, 1949, he succeeded in renting a large studio in St Ives, and so at last could expand. Before long he was producing the large-scale works that were to win him prizes at international competitions and secure his future.

Shortly before his father's death he had visited Brittany for the first time and been deeply impressed by the landscape, the people, the architecture and the megaliths, though the immediate outcome was no more than a handful of drawings. The next spring, though, he travelled to Tuscany specifically to make drawings, and this proved to be the start of a remarkable flowering – a quarter-century in which he made hundreds of drawings of landscape, still life and architecture. Unequalled in their verve and subtlety, they are among his most personal expressions and a major part of his oeuvre.

1950 was also to be a turning-point in Ben Nicholson's personal life. His association with Barbara Hepworth, which had begun in the early 1930s – in the heady days of self-discovery and participation in the modern movement – had now run its course and ended in acrimony. Whatever the rights and wrongs on either side, this too was for him a new beginning (though it was several years before he again found happiness in a new relationship). Now approaching sixty, he felt (and behaved) half his age.

A fresh commitment to the carved and painted relief followed a little later. After six years away from this medium, which he had made peculiarly his own, he took it up again in 1953 and soon developed its expressive potentialities far beyond anything he had done previously. These later, so-called primitive, reliefs are his most original achievement – a synthesis and a summation of earlier work – the culmination of his career, as he himself recognized in a letter he wrote in May 1962 to his friend and long-time champion, Herbert Read: 'The reliefs – both the white ones & the later primitive reliefs – are what I'd choose to stand or fall by (– the reliefs, then the dwgs, then the ptgs).'

drawing and carving

This exhibition focuses on the parallel and complementary activities of drawing and carving which engrossed Nicholson in the years between 1950 and 1975, the period of his fullest artistic maturity. (Paintings of his on canvas become rare after the mid-1950s and cease altogether in the mid-1960s.) Drawing and carving are, in fact, very closely associated throughout Nicholson's career. By the early 1930s he had evolved his own essentially linear approach to drawing, in which the subtle inflection of the enclosing line is made to suggest volume and modelling without the aid of illusionistic shading or stippling. The tautness of the pencil line and its sensitively varying width and speed give the impression that it is carved or incised into the paper. And this is precisely what does happen in Nicholson's paintings on board or canvas: the pencil or pointed stylus both draws and carves through the paint (sometimes to reveal the white priming) whether it be the outlines of mug, jug and bottle, or the complicated geometry of a St Ives roofscape, or free arabesques with a rhythm and life of their own.

The closest identity of drawing with carving occurs in Nicholson's print-making – linocuts between 1926 and 1933, drypoints in 1948 and in the 1950s, and most importantly in the context of this exhibition, the one hundred and thirty etchings made in the years 1965–9. Nicholson's etchings, by his own admission, are really carved drawings: he enjoyed the sensation of cutting into the plate but otherwise he was drawing on it just as he would with a pencil on paper. He had little interest in, and never troubled to master, the techniques special to the etching process. Though extremely demanding in his requirements and critical of results, he was content to leave the actual printing in the (initially quite inexperienced) hands of François Lafranca.

For Nicholson it was never enough simply to apply paint to canvas or pencil to paper. Long before he ever carved a relief he was making and carving frames for his pictures, and always enjoyed any job that involved simple carpentry – a mirror-frame, a doll's house, a pencil box or a toy. And the first carved relief of December 1933 looks much like part of some homemade board-game. Yet only a few months later the deliberate lack of finish and drab colour had, like a cygnet into a swan, metamorphosed into a serene, all white composition in which square and circle are held in tense equilibrium and the subtly gradated depths of carved mahogany reflect the changing light with shadows that swell and narrow like the vital pencil lines of a Nicholson drawing.

1950-55 – drawings

In May 1950 Nicholson set off for a three-week drawing trip in Tuscany. In charge of all the arrangements and of the driving was his friend and patron Cyril Reddihough (1903-2002), whom he had known since 1927. With his imperturbable good-humour, modesty, kindness, enthusiasm and practicality, 'Redd' was the perfect travelling-companion for the volatile and exacting Nicholson. More importantly, it was he who, recognizing Nicholson's exceptional ability as a draughtsman, had encouraged him to develop this aspect of his art. Apart from a mastery of line, there are in his drawing qualities of wit, poetry, spontaneity and, at times, of childishness, which make them perhaps the closest reflection of his personality. Stimulated by this encouragement, Nicholson made a series of drawings so far unprecedented both in quality and in quantity.

They made San Gimignano their headquarters. In **Single tower, San Gimignano** (cat. 5) we look out through the open doors and shutters of Nicholson's hotel bedroom to the balcony outside; beyond it, to one of the mediaeval fortified towers for which San Gimignano is famous; then back again indoors to savour the detail of the taps on the washbasin, the keys, the clasps, the doorhandles, the minimal triangles of shade in the slats of the shutters, the virtuoso stringing on the back of the chair; and then the tiny landscape squeezed between shutter and tower. In the drawing made three days earlier (cat. 2) the Tuscan landscape is all but shut out by a semi-abstract pattern of roofs and towers with the simplified outlines of a jug and goblet superimposed in the foreground. One step further and Nicholson would fuse still-life and architectural elements into a self-existent composition in which line and shape and space play against each other in an endless rhythm and metamorphosis. By contrast, **La Buca** (cat. 4) is a relatively straightforward, relaxed

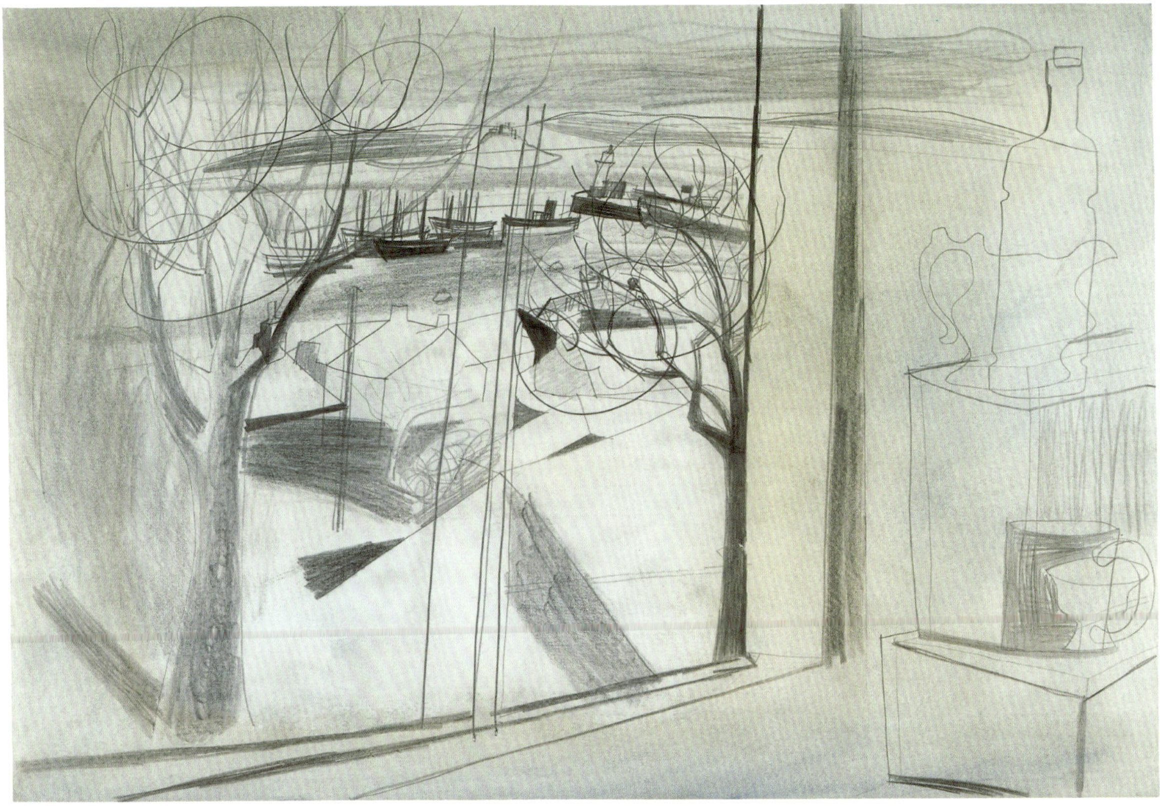

April 11 1950 (Newlyn)
35.5 x 51 cm (cat. 1)

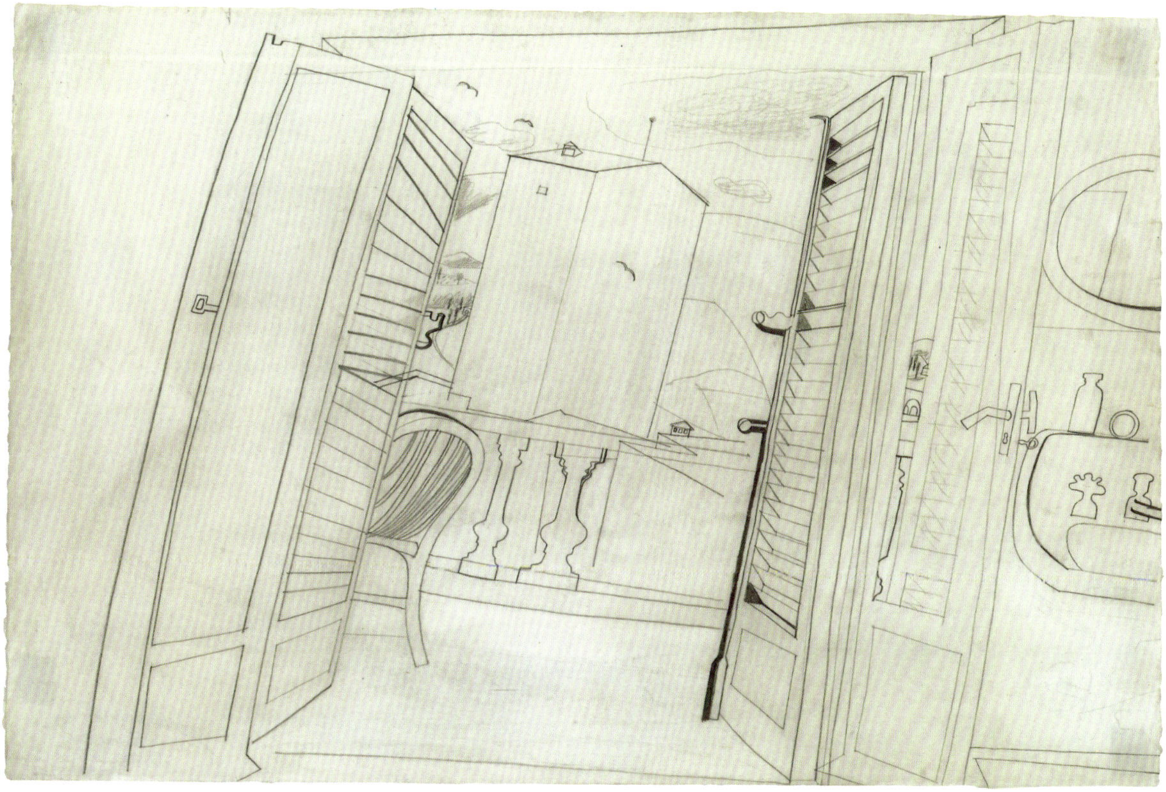

May 24 1950 (single tower, San Gimignano)
39 x 58 cm (cat. 5)

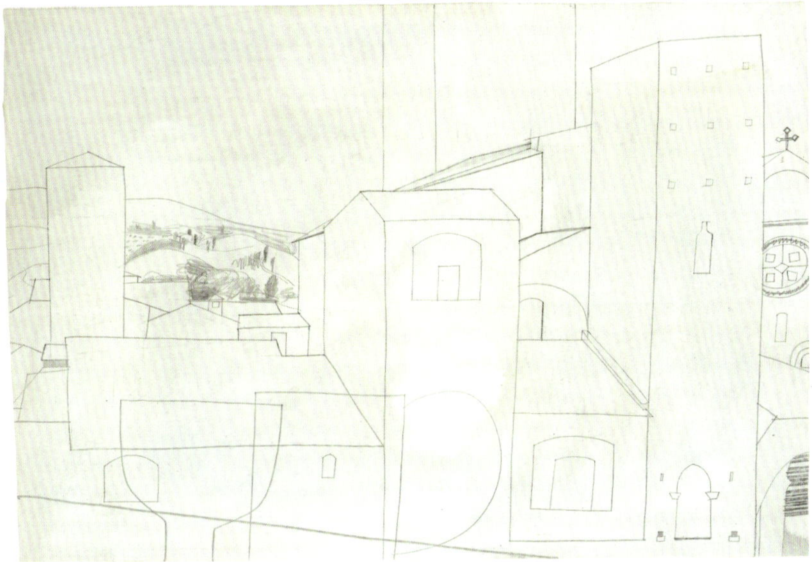

May 21 1950 (San Gimignano)
35.5 x 51 cm (cat. 2)

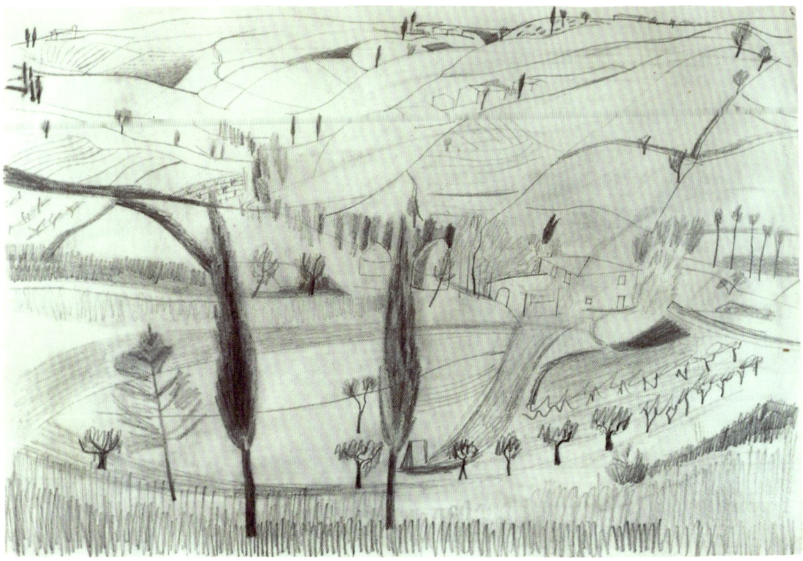

May 22 1950 (La Buca, Tuscany)
35.5 x 51 cm (cat. 4)

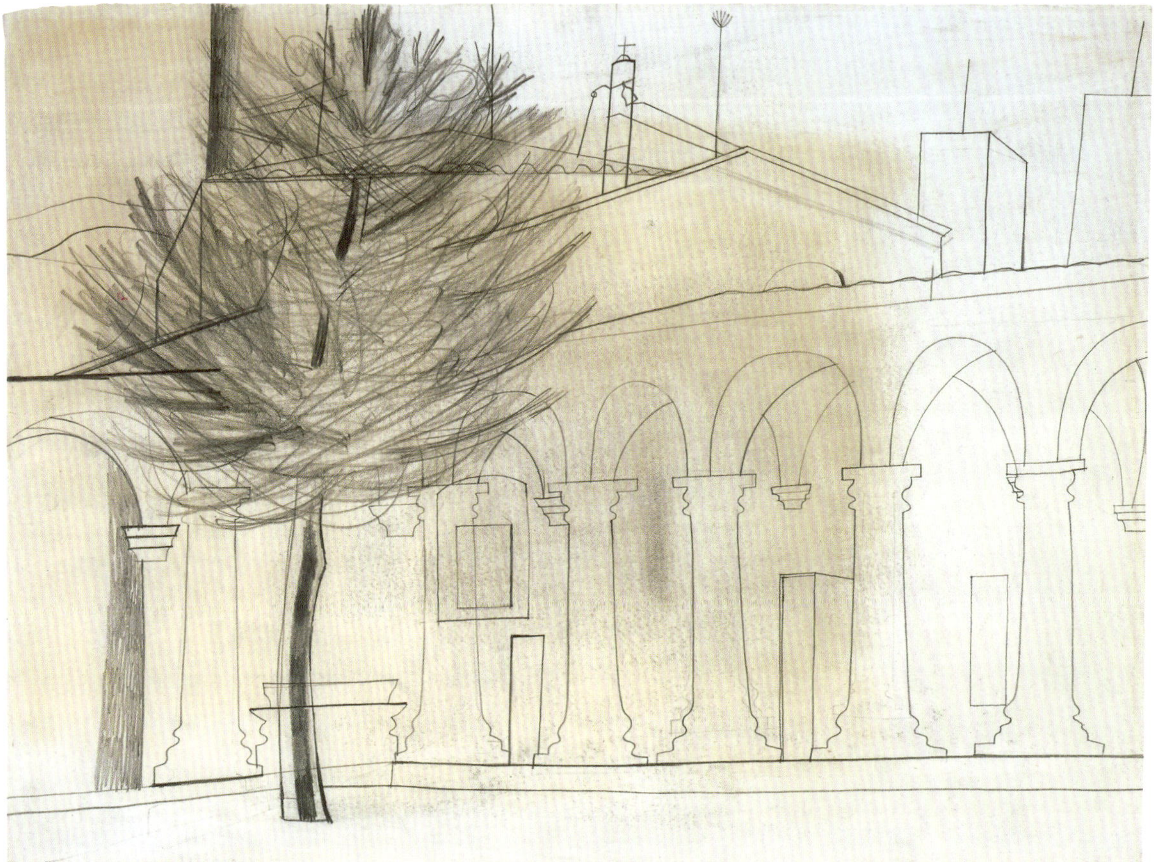

May 22 1950 (cloisters, San Gimignano)
38.1 x 50.8 cm (cat. 3)

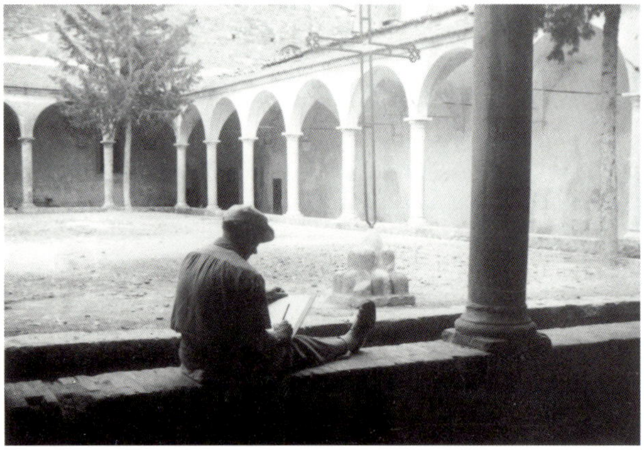

Ben Nicholson drawing in the cloisters, San Gimignano, 1950

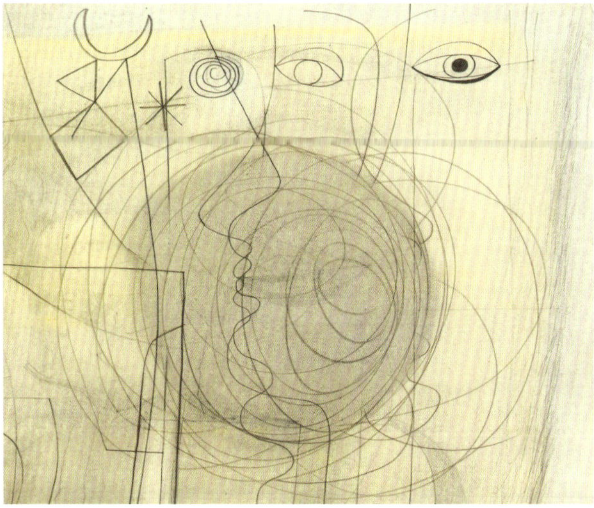

May 12 1954 (portrait of the artist)
29 x 34 cm (cat. 10)

notation of the Tuscan hill-country, harking back to the sketches Nicholson made in Cornwall in the 1940s. The liveliest of his landscape drawings nearly always have some architectural element in them that acts as a foil: a tension is set up between rectilinear, 'abstract' shapes and curvilinear, 'natural' ones. This playing-off of the man-made against the natural is typified in **Cloisters, San Gimignano** (cat. 3) where the regular rhythm of the arcading contrasts with the wild scribble of the tree.

A similar idea animates a small drawing made back in St Ives the following year (cat. 6). Two thirds of the space are filled with free variations on jug, cup and goblet, which keep the eye in perpetual motion. Then, looking out from behind the curtainlike dividing line, we get a view of a church-steeple, some roofs and a ship in the bay. While the spacious rhythm of the still life indoors is carried over into the steeple and body of the church outside, the houses and ship beyond are in Nicholson's faux-naif, Toytown style which ultimately stems from illustrations he made in 1937-8 for an episodic story he used to tell his children about the doings of two horses, George and Rufus. Many of Nicholson's Cornish landscapes dating from 1939-46 have a strong element of this 'nursery realism' which occasionally resurfaces, as here, in later years.

Entirely different, and still more closely connected with the 1930s, is the **Portrait of the artist** (cat. 10) contributed to a series of self-

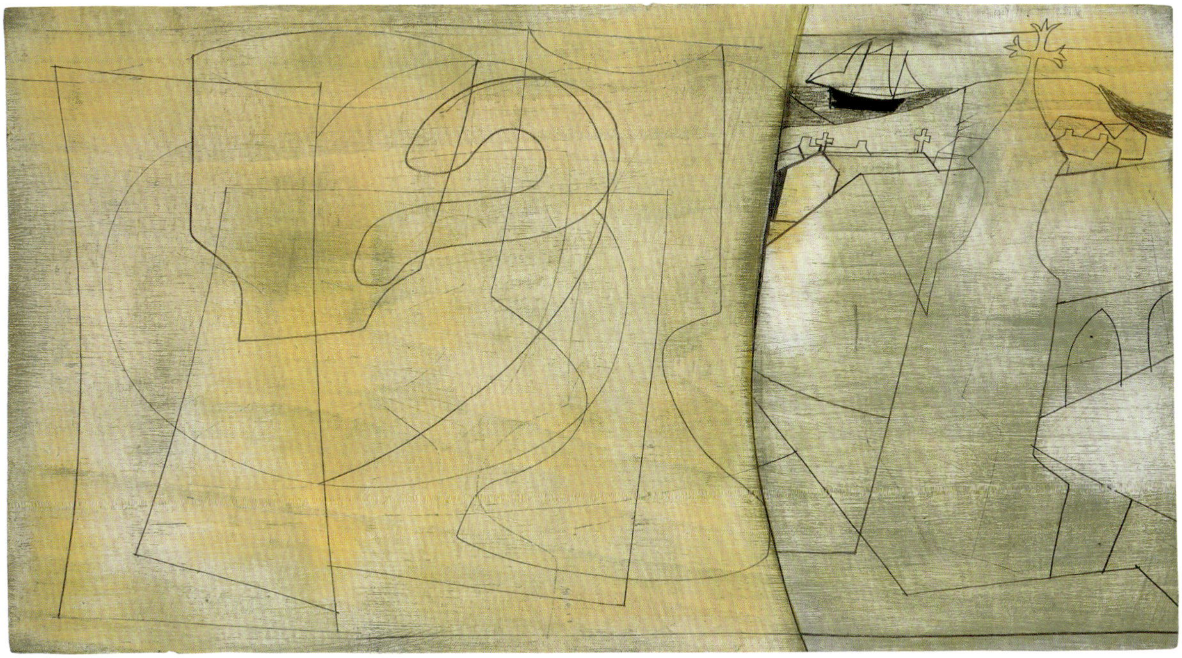

October 1951 (still life, steeple & ship)
20 x 35.5 cm (cat. 6)

portraits commissioned from British artists by *Art News and Review* between 1949 and 1960. It was published in July 1954 to coincide with the showing of Nicholson's work at the XXVII Venice Biennale. Having little or no interest in drawing likenesses, and strongly disliking any cult of the artist's personality, Nicholson was bound to sidestep straight self-portraiture. He did so by reverting to an enigmatic, only partially revealing, style, evolved under the influence of Miró in 1933, in the early days of his love for Barbara Hepworth, when he made a number of double-portraits out of their intertwined profiles. Though this drawing sits outside the mainstream of Nicholson's development, as a self-portrait it is, indirectly, revealing.

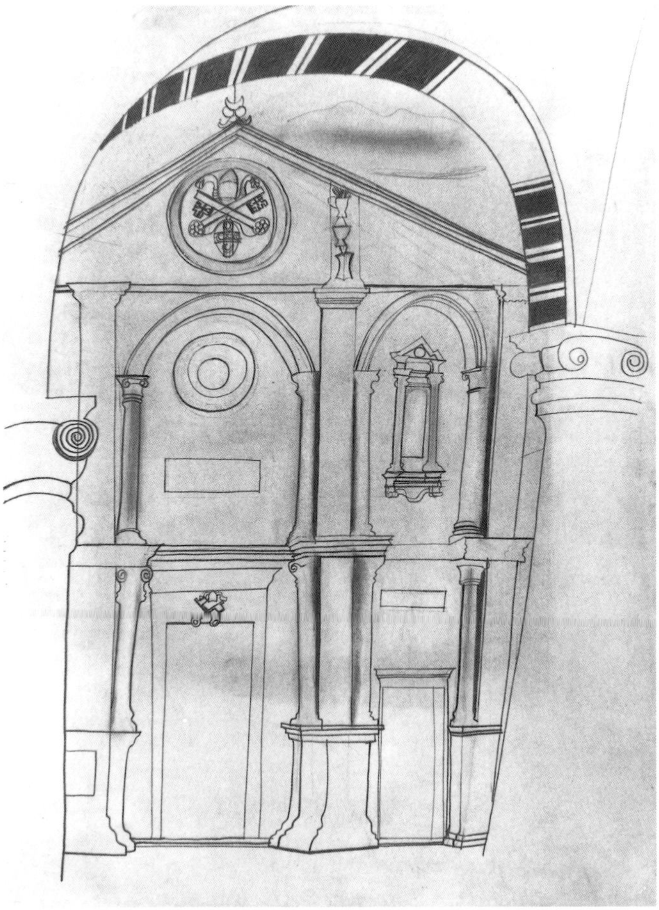

October 5 1955 (cathedral, Pienza)
53 x 40.7 cm (cat. 13)

On a second trip to Italy with Reddihough in 1955 Nicholson worked his way south from Tuscany, through Umbria, to Rome. From the rich harvest that resulted one drawing of architecture and one of landscape are representative. **Cathedral, Pienza** (cat. 13) shows Nicholson's method of capturing the spirit of a building by a combination of bold omission and selective detail, often with a visual joke (note the left-hand pillar supporting the pediment). Beside the controlled economy of line in this architectural drawing Nicholson demonstrates several other ways of using a pencil in **Metallic landscape, Buonconvento** (cat. 12). The first and

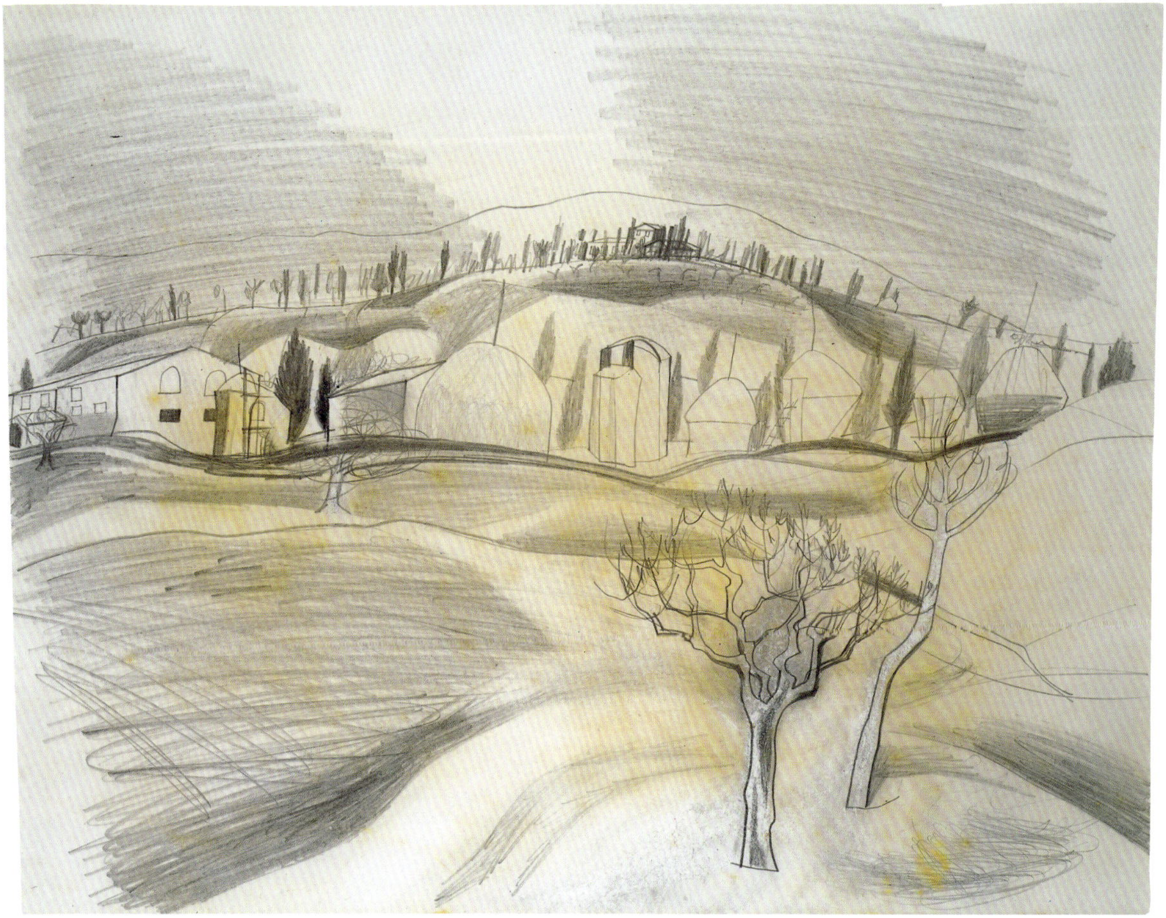

October 2 1955 (metallic landscape, Buonconvento)
36 x 43.9 cm (cat. 12)

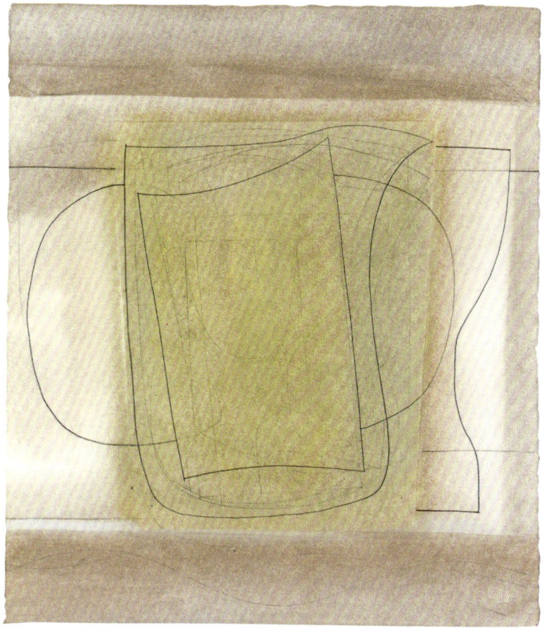

1968 (green still life)
49 x 41 cm (cat. 36)

opposite
1957 (Rievaulx Abbey)
35.5 x 48.2 cm (cat. 16)

most obvious characteristic is that all the pencil marks are frankly pencil marks: there is no attempt at concealment or illusionism, and yet a specific landscape, maybe also an imminent thunderstorm, are vividly evoked. The colour wash adds body and character to the drawing. It was a practice Nicholson adopted in the late 1940s when he was beginning to take his drawings more seriously. He would prepare in advance a good number of sheets with oil washes of varying shape, colour and opacity, without any idea for what subjects they might eventually serve as background. Later he would select the one most appropriate to what he wanted to draw. Like the priming on a canvas, the wash then served as a stimulus, a given situation needing to be turned to the drawing's advantage. The oil wash and its relation to the drawing can be so subtle, particularly in Nicholson's later drawings, that it is often hard to believe that the wash already existed before any thought of the drawing. Nicholson did occasionally add colour to a finished drawing, but this was rare and he certainly never added an oil wash since it would have eradicated the pencil lines, as can be seen in **1968 (green still life)** (cat. 36) where, for deliberate effect, he has painted over lines, allowing only their ghosts to show through.

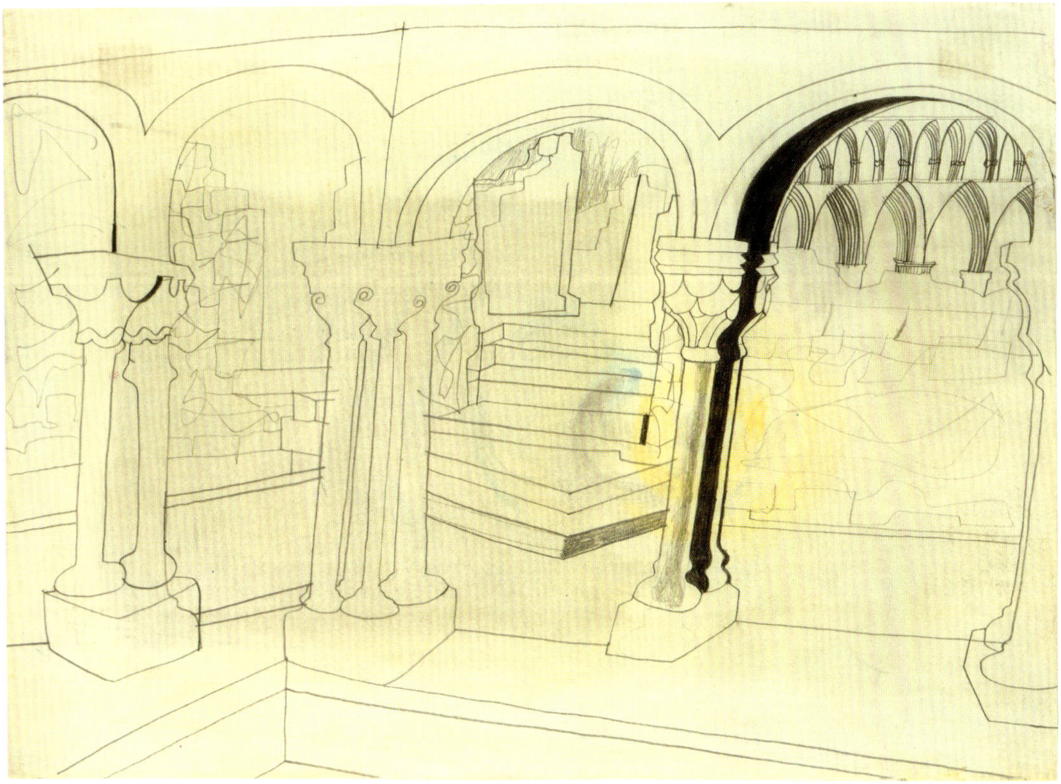

1957-8 – a new life

In May 1957 Nicholson met Felicitas Vogler, a freelance radio journalist and photographer, who had come to St Ives to do a feature on the artists' community for Bavarian radio. Two months later they were married. (**1957 (Rievaulx Abbey)** (cat. 16) was drawn while they were on honeymoon in Yorkshire.) Nicholson, even before remarrying, had intended to leave St Ives, and in March 1958 he moved with 'Feli' to the Ticino on the Italian border of Switzerland, where he was to live for the next thirteen years. In April 1961 they settled into their own specially commissioned house on a steep, wooded hillside, 1400 feet above Lake Maggiore, with views across the lake to Ascona, Locarno and the mountains beyond. Not only the landscape but the climate and the quality of light were invigorating, and the whole feel of the place was further charged with memories going back to his first visit to the Ticino in the winter of 1912-3 as well as his long stays there with his first wife, Winifred, in the early 1920s.

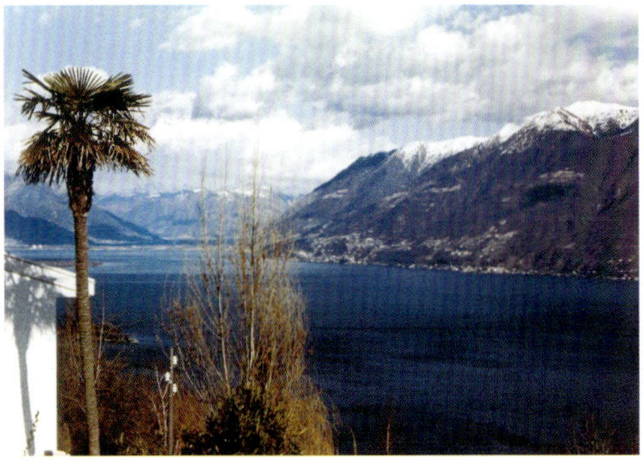

View from Casa alla Rocca

Living in the centre of Europe was an incentive to travel – to Brittany, the Loire valley, Provence, the Pyrenees, Portugal and, most frequently, over the border to Tuscany, Umbria, Rome, Apulia. Beside the new motifs discovered on these travels there was the stimulus of making contact with other artists. Foremost, perhaps, was Mark Tobey, at that time living in Basel, with whom he felt in personal sympathy, and whose work he admired greatly. He also made friends with Julius Bissier (who spent his last years near Ascona), attracted by the texture of his paintings on fine linen. Both Hans Arp and Hans Richter lived nearby and occasionally exchanged visits with Nicholson, while regular attendance at the Venice Biennale and at the Documenta exhibitions in Kassel resulted in further contacts – with Pierre Soulages, Serge Poliakoff, Alberto Burri, Zoran Music – and the opportunity to see and sometimes admire a wide range of contemporary work.

Altogether the move to Switzerland, away from what had become for him the stifling parochialism of St Ives, opened up new vistas for Nicholson, released new energies and inaugurated a decade in which his work would attain the greatest power and profundity.

1958-71 – drawings & painted reliefs

In the two-room Casa Ticinella, just below the church at Ronco, Nicholson's first address on arrival in Switzerland, he was restricted to making small-scale works – drawings based on his favourite still-life objects. **April 1958 (Prato)** (cat. 17) will have been among the earliest of these line drawings, which were to proliferate over the next few years, in pencil or in ink, with or without heightening in colour, on paper or on board. Note how in **Prato** the irregular shape of the paper determines the shape of the drawing and greatly adds to its vitality as an object. In the past Nicholson had achieved something of this effect by tilting the drawing at an angle to the rectangular sheet of paper (as in **1950 (single tower, San Gimignano)** (cat. 5)). Cutting the paper

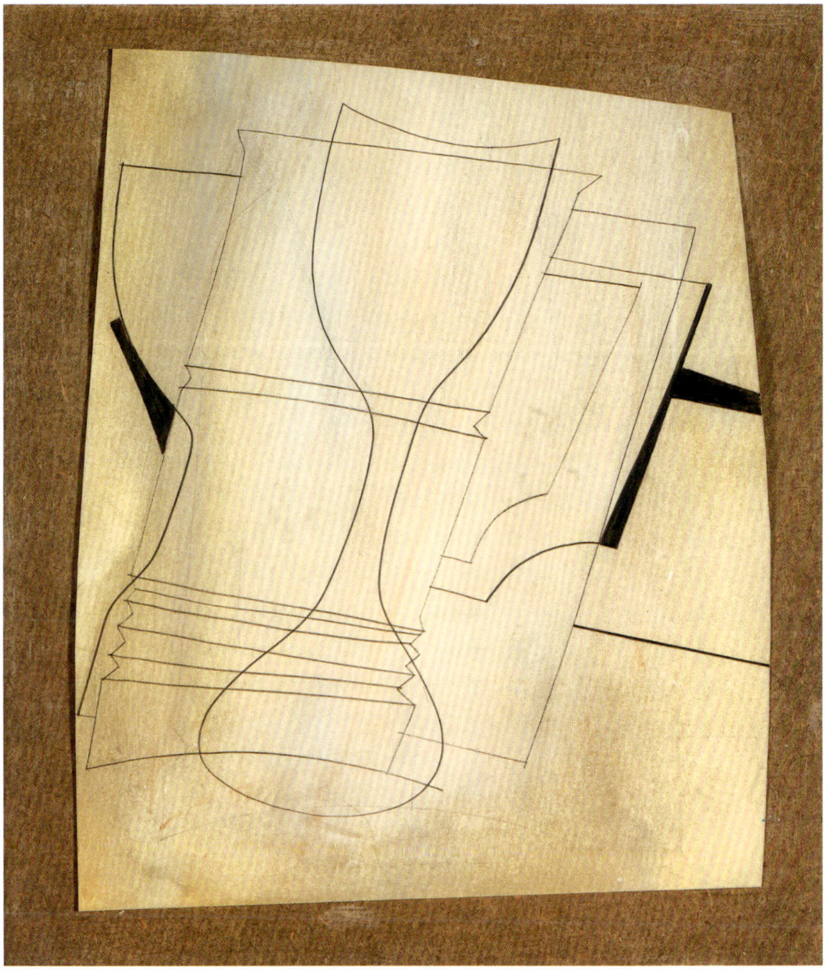

April 1958 (Prato)
34 x 29.5 cm (cat. 17)

itself into an irregular shape (and getting away from the convention of the strict rectangle) made it part of the total expression of the drawing. Gradually he introduced these curved, tensile shapes into his reliefs, with even greater dramatic effect.

Goblet and blue square and **Alnwick** (cat. 22, cat. 21), both made in June 1961, the same size and in the same medium of oil and pencil on board, are companion pieces. In **Alnwick** the

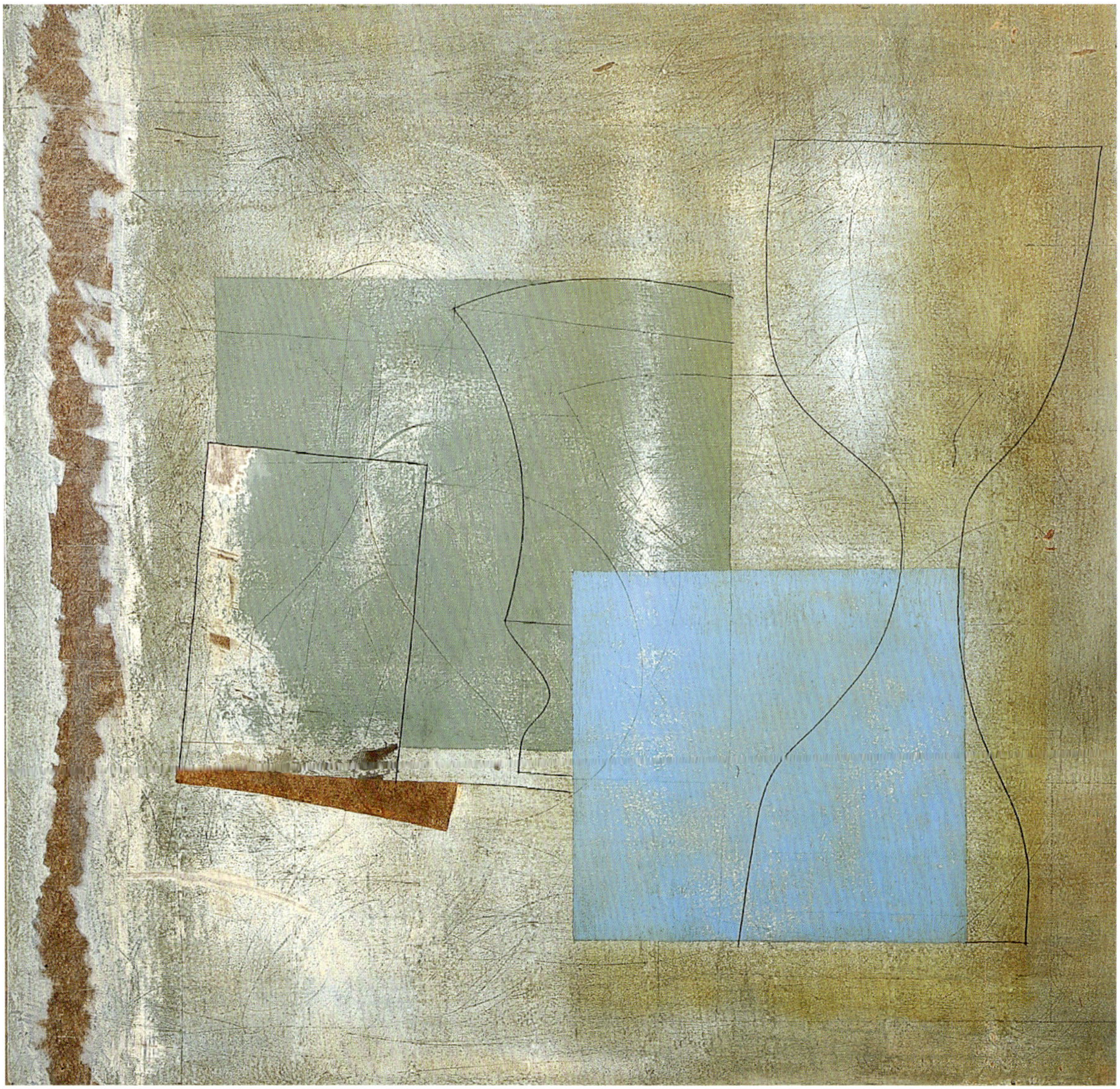

June 1961 (goblet and blue square)
80 x 80 cm (cat. 22)

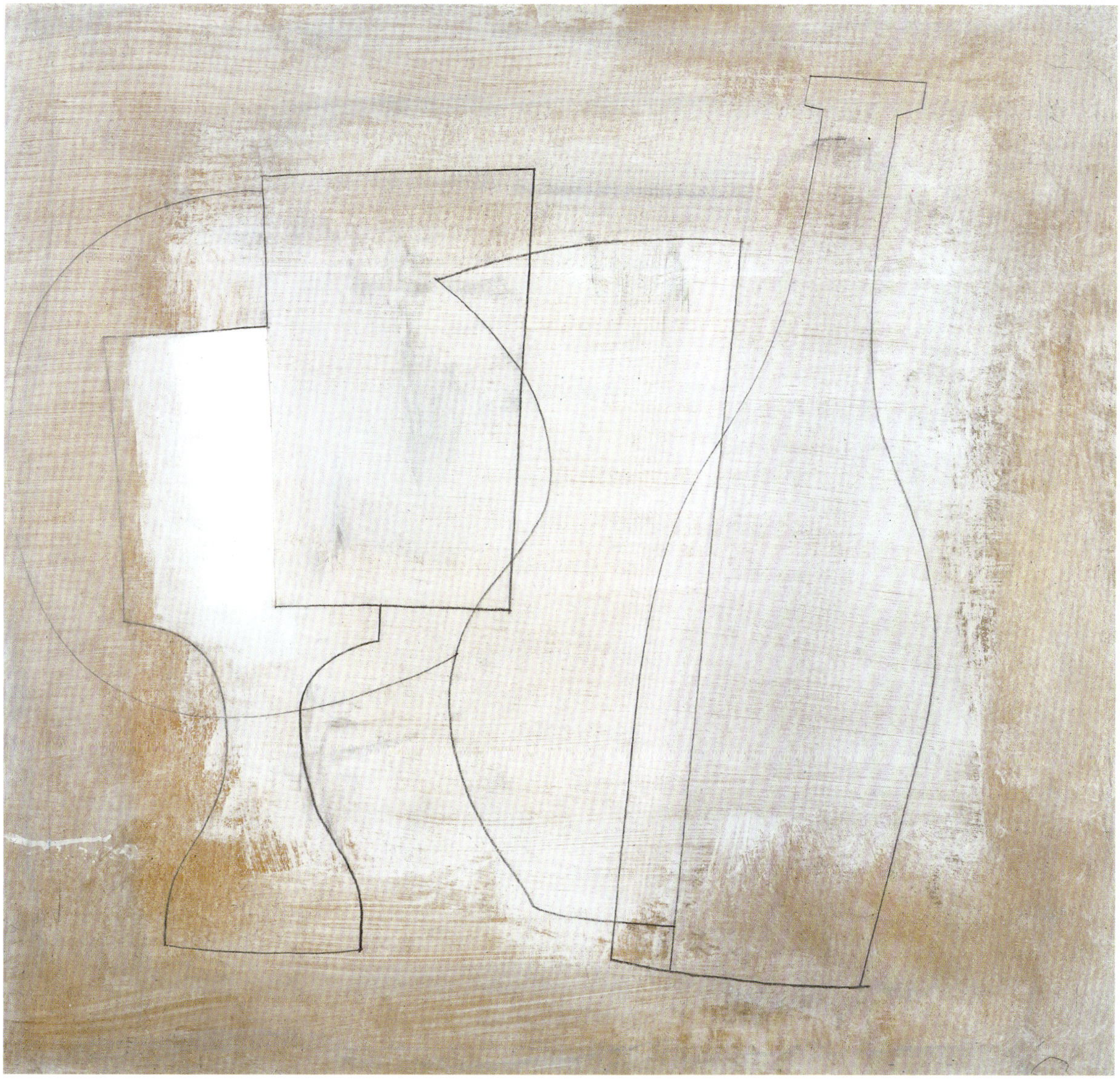

June 1961 (Alnwick)
80 x 82.5 cm (cat. 21)

jaunty carafe ought to be concealing the handle and right-hand side of the jug, if they existed. Facing these is a goblet partially overlaid by a trapezoid (Nicholson's sign for a cup), the sweeping curve of whose handle has broken free only to collide with the outline of the half-jug. This typically playful, typically virtuosic fantasia on a still-life theme is given an extra dimension by the veils of oil wash that create luminosity, mystery and a sense of infinite space. It is no surprise that when Nicholson visited Mark Rothko at his studio in New York in 1965, this should have been the work Rothko chose in exchange for one of his own. Nicholson greatly admired Rothko's work, probably seeing in it some affinity with his own, and regretted that the Rothko he chose could not be a monumental one.

Turning to **Goblet and blue square** – an hour-glass goblet takes the place of the carafe in **Alnwick** and this time, without any ambiguity of concealment, the beaker in the centre is truncated. To its left we have the same rectangle + semicircle = mug, but facing the other way. These are the main outlines, but there are many others half-obliterated in or under the paint, ghostly echoes of earlier still-life confrontations. Opposed to the perfect clarity of the goblet on the right is the ragged strip of burnt sienna down the left of the board. The thin veil of white overlaying it teases us into thinking the support is paper, torn so as to reveal the board beneath. The beauty of imperfection – of the worn, torn, scuffed or abraded surface – is central to Nicholson's aesthetic and offsets the clear perfection of his line. Sometimes an imperfection can be the starting-point of a work. Accidents such as blots, tears or discolouration were welcome. For instance, the dent (he would have called it an acci dent) in the top left-hand edge of the paper on which he drew **1970 (Lavenham)** (cat. 41 *overpage*) or the mended tear in the centre of **1950 (San Gimignano)** (cat. 2). If there was no ready-made imperfection, then he would manufacture one, as here in **Goblet and blue square**, to heighten the object-quality of the work and to bring it closer to something natural. So often in his later reliefs we see the surface of the board scoured and then suffused with the colour of earth, stone, moss or terracotta. Here the extreme of aesthetic refinement partly rejoins, partly transcends the natural, as in a raku tea-bowl or in the disposition of rock, moss and gravel within the rectangle of a Zen temple garden.

In his explorations Nicholson moves instinctively from one medium to another: from the irreducible simplicity of **July 1962 (white jug)** (cat. 26), consisting of a few pencil-lines on a sheet of white paper, to **October 1962 (three circles)** (cat. 27), where the texture, colour and suggestion of planes at different depths makes us momentarily uncertain whether it may not be a relief, to the point when cutting a line into the surface of a board rather than simply drawing a line on a piece of paper makes us apprehend the work simply and directly as a material object with its own reality, and at the same time effectively banishes illusionism: the circle really is on a deeper level than the surrounding rectangle. This and the possibility of varying texture by scraping and cutting the board were always to allure Nicholson, as was the much slower tempo of carving a relief, compared with the swift spontaneity of a pencil drawing. In the long hours of concentrated effort, physical and mental, he could gradually come closer to a realization of his idea, go deeper into his sense of a reality underlying outward appearances, and so hint at the universal, whereas his drawings usually remain tied, however loosely, to the particular.

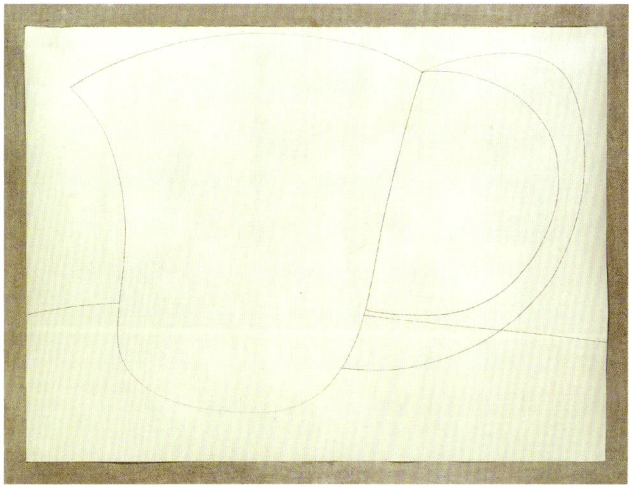

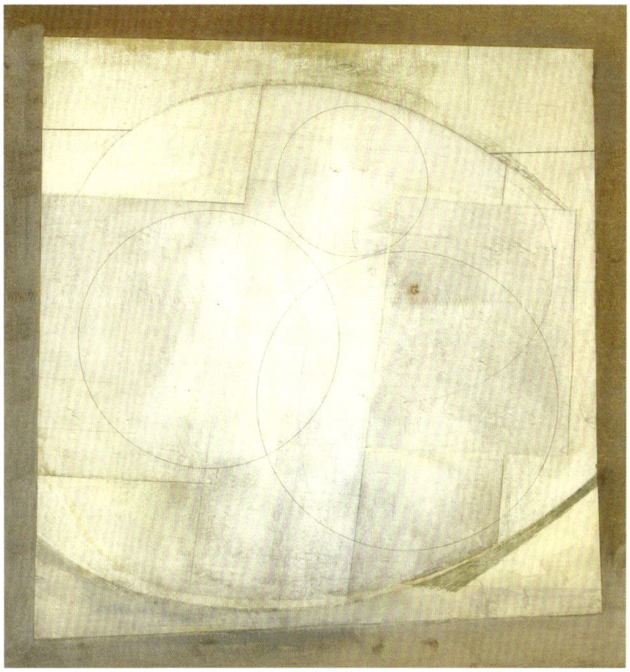

July 1962 (white jug)
49.5 x 61.5 cm (cat. 26)

October 1962 (three circles)
35.6 x 33 cm (cat. 27)

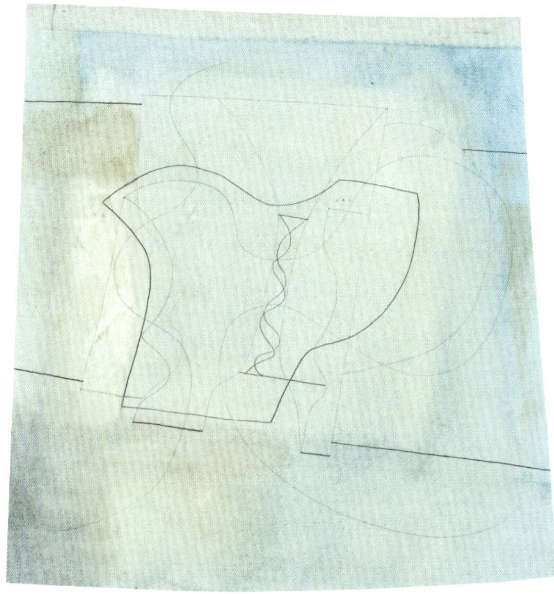

August 1972
(still life with some blue)
38 x 35 cm (cat. 46)

opposite
1970 (Lavenham)
62 x 50 cm (cat. 41)

Many of Nicholson's still-life drawings and paintings have place-names for title, often because they seem to inhabit or to suggest landscape. Here the connexion is more specific: Nicholson bought the wine-glass, portrayed in between the two goblets, at Lavenham in Suffolk, a year before returning to live permanently in England. The spiral twist in the stem clearly attracted him and appears in more than a dozen drawings made in the next three years, including **August 1972 (still life with some blue)** (cat. 46). In both drawings the movement and speed of the lines that define the still-life objects and grow out of them create a sensation of freedom, lightness and soaring flight. These were Nicholson's ideals. All is perfectly controlled, all is lucid, yet mysterious and without end. Note, in **1970 (Lavenham)**, how the sheet of paper, beside the nick in its top-left edge, is not a perfect rectangle, and how the mount has become part of the work: it has been scoured with sandpaper then lightly brushed over with a wash of white so as to produce the weathered, stone-like texture often seen in the primitive reliefs, eg **1966 (Saronikos)** (cat. 31). This contrast of texture and its suggestion of the natural world and the time-worn add a further dimension to our perception of the drawing.

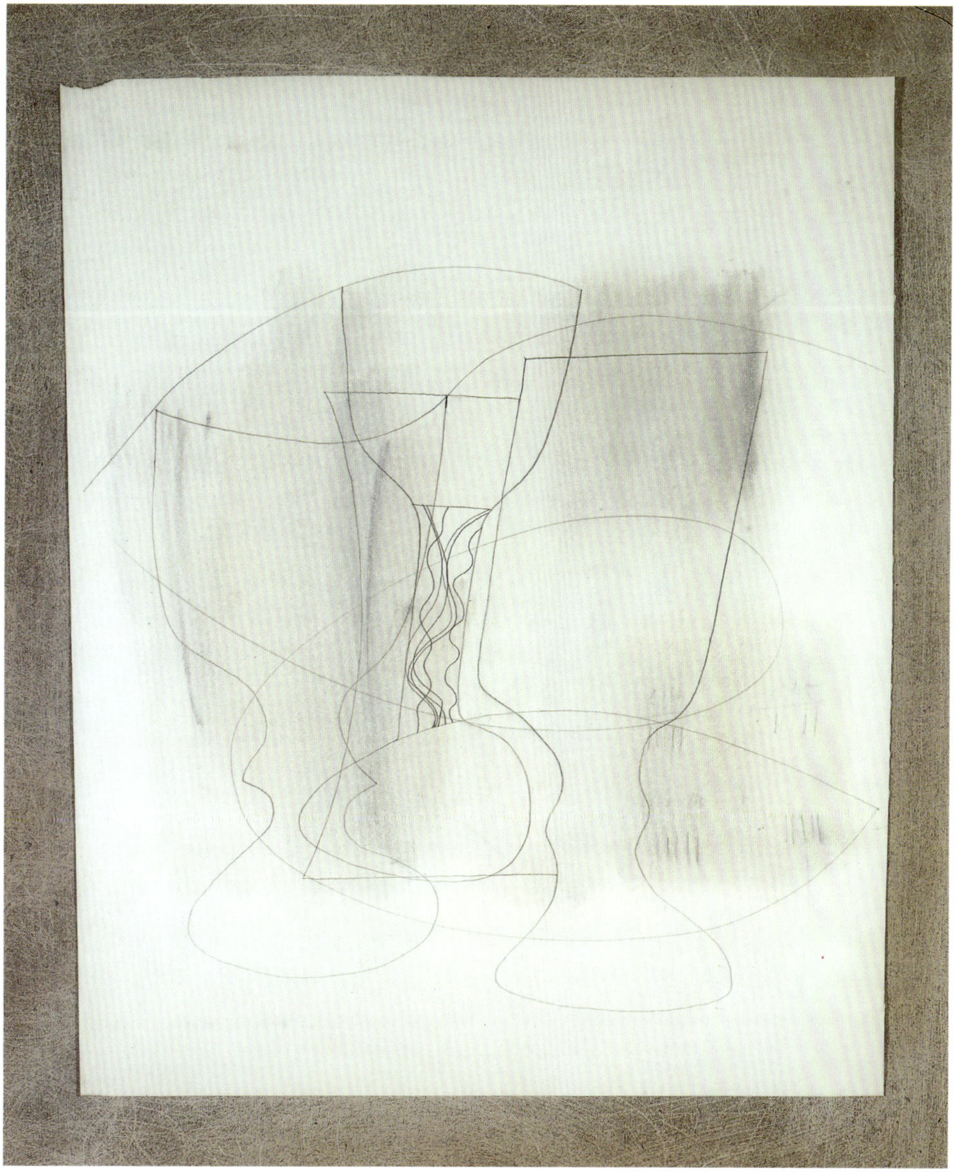

Returning to the medium of the painted relief in 1953, after an interval of six years, Nicholson gradually enlarged the scope of its reference. At the deepest level, the grandeur of the mountains and the lake, which he looked at every day, directly affected his conception of the relief, as did memories of landscape and experiences in landscape elsewhere. But from a purely formal viewpoint too the transformation was radical. Hitherto the straight lines that he carved had nearly always been orthogonal, but now he increasingly introduced slanting lines and trapezoid forms, thereby altering the whole character and dynamic of the work. In the earlier reliefs circles, squares and rectangles were ordered into serene equilibrium. Any potential clash of forms was suppressed or eliminated. Now the opposing forces were allowed more freedom, more dramatic interaction, contained within a tauter equilibrium, though diagonal lines and trapezoid forms necessarily suggest movement beyond the rectilinear bounds of the frame. **May 22 1956 (hendrifter)** (cat. 14), which, less mysteriously but more graphically, also goes by the name of **Magnet**, exemplifies in miniature this clash of opposites, while in **1966 (Saronikos)** (cat. 31) a different dynamic situation is presented, this time on a monumental scale and heightened by the dramatic use of red.

In these later reliefs we see Nicholson constantly exploring and developing the potentialities of colour and texture just as much as form. It is as if all the subtle gradations of colour, tone and texture that he registered while drawing landscape and architecture were stored away, later to find expression in his carved surfaces where colour is not simply brushed onto the surface of the board but is made to seem indivisible from it. These formal and technical developments go hand in hand with Nicholson's expanding range of motifs and with his desire to make his work as inclusive a response to life as possible.

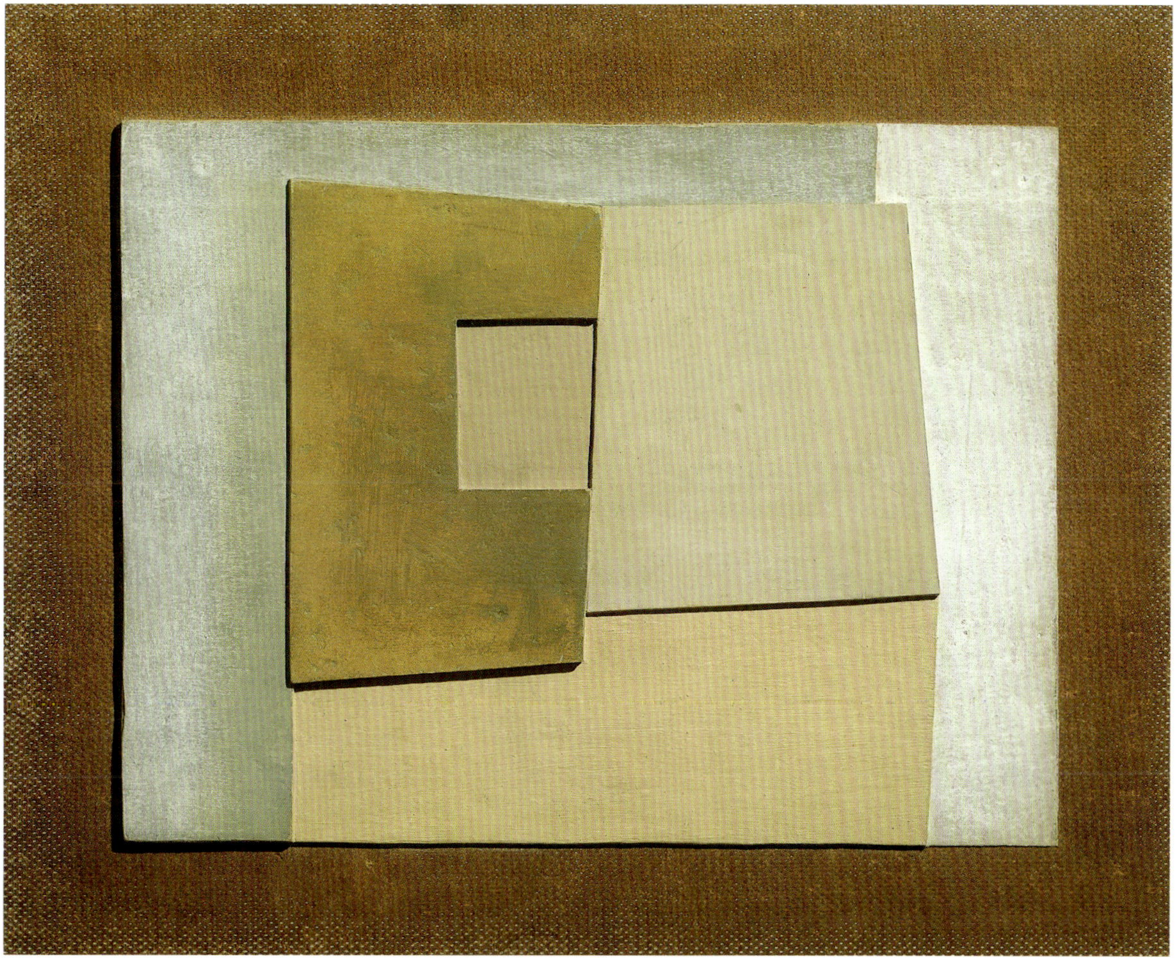

May 22 1956 (hendrifter)
36 x 43 cm (cat. 14)

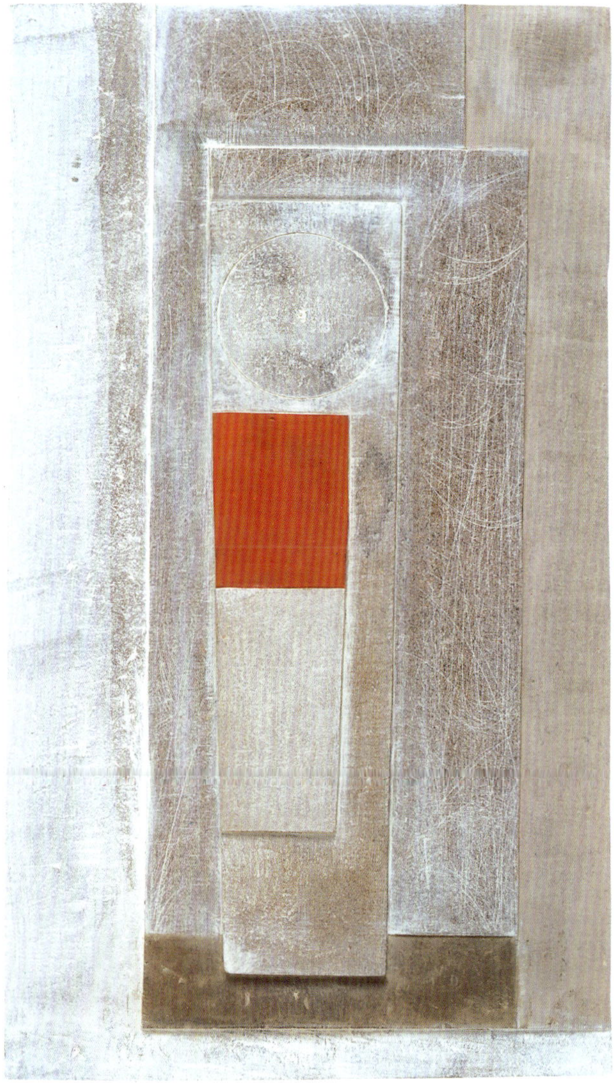

1966 (vertical wall)
43.2 x 26.7 cm (cat. 33)

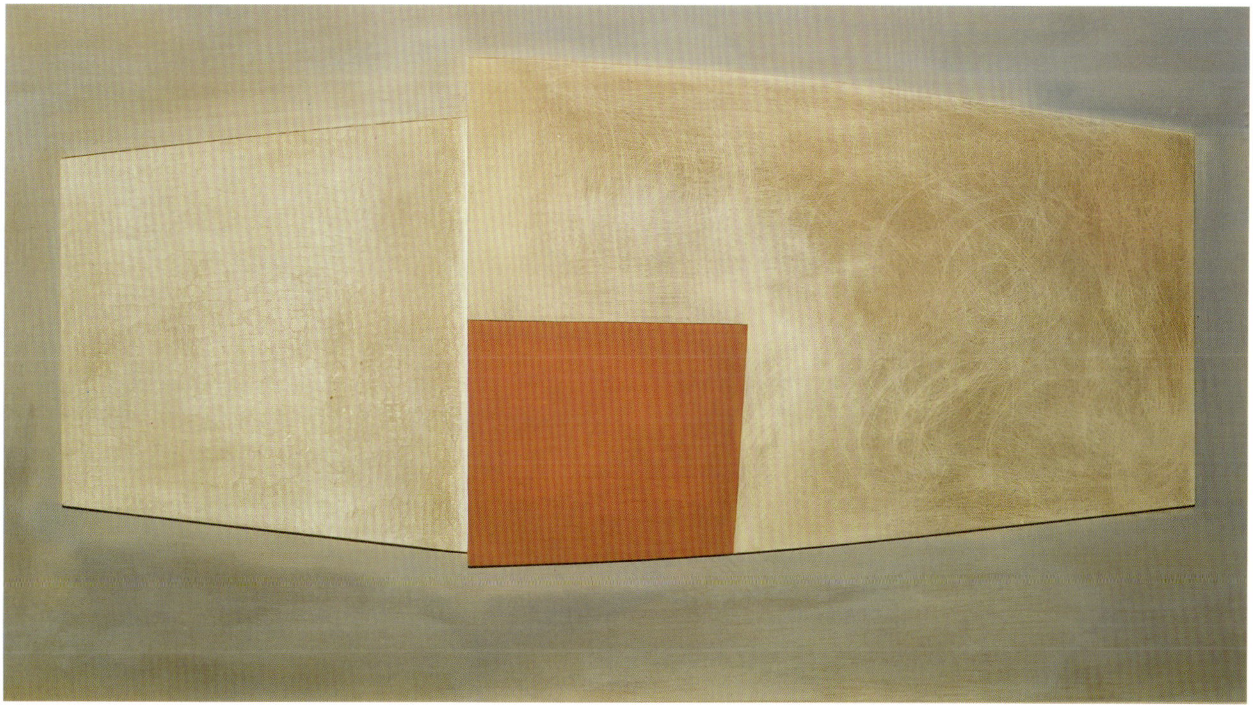

1966 (Saronikos)
74 x 128 cm (cat. 31)

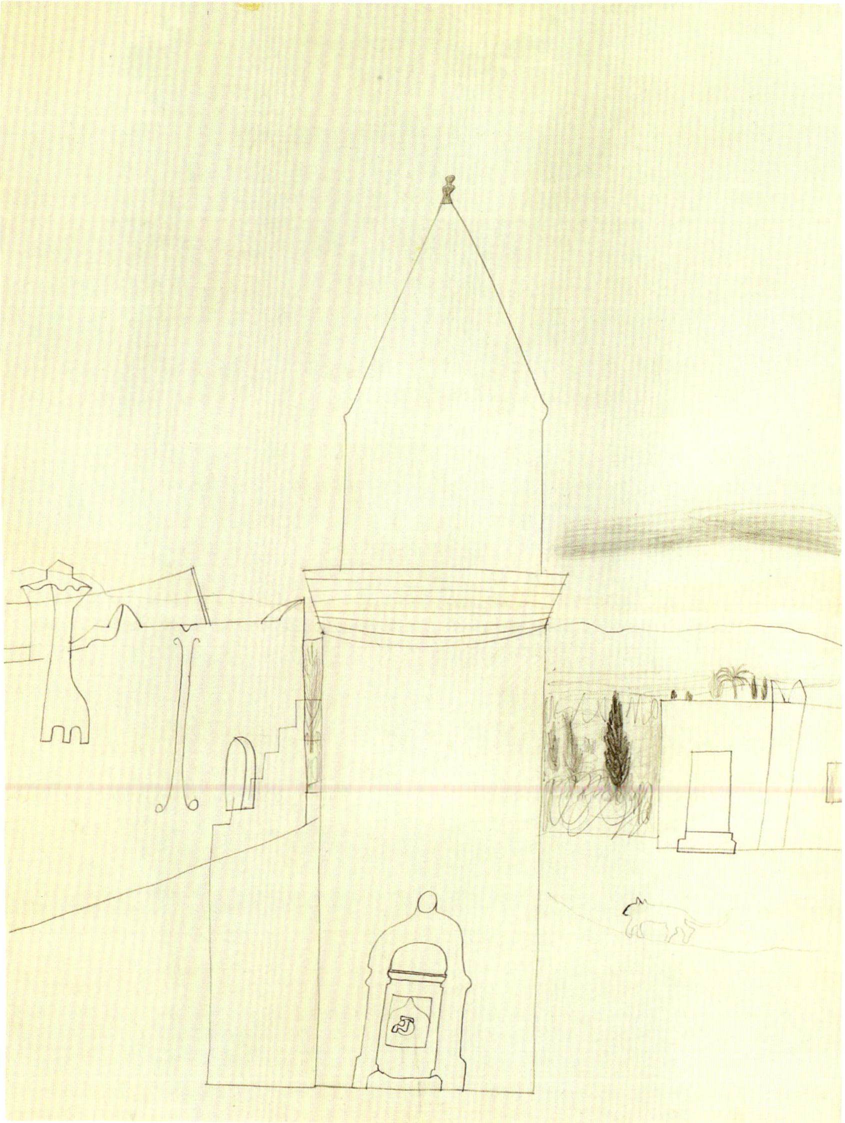

April 1959 (Kos)
48 x 35.2 cm (cat. 20)

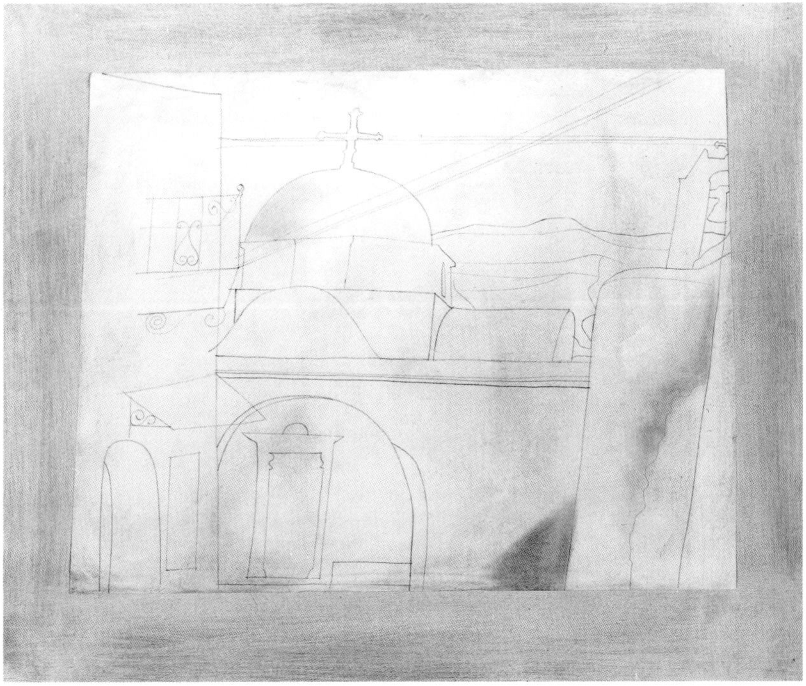

September 1961 (Paros chapel)
40 x 49.5 cm (cat. 23)

After Italy it was Greece and the Aegean which most inspired Nicholson. A preliminary reconnaissance in April 1959 was followed by five more visits over the next fourteen years. He returned more than once to certain sites that had a particular significance for him, such as Mycenae, Epidauros, Olympia and the islands of Aegina, Paros and Kos. On Kos, only a few miles from the Turkish mainland, he was attracted by an old minaret and managed to draw it despite the distraction of children at play and passing tourists. The drawing (cat. 20) has several Nicholson hallmarks: large empty areas contrasted with small passages of intense detail, such as the tap and basin at the foot of the rather squat minaret and the landscape of olive trees with one palm to reinforce the slightly exotic locale on the edge of the Islamic world; a cat, like nearly all Nicholson's animals drawn with defiant naivety, and to the left of the minaret, some quirks and ambiguities in the architecture. By contrast, **September 1961 (Paros chapel)** (cat. 23) is a

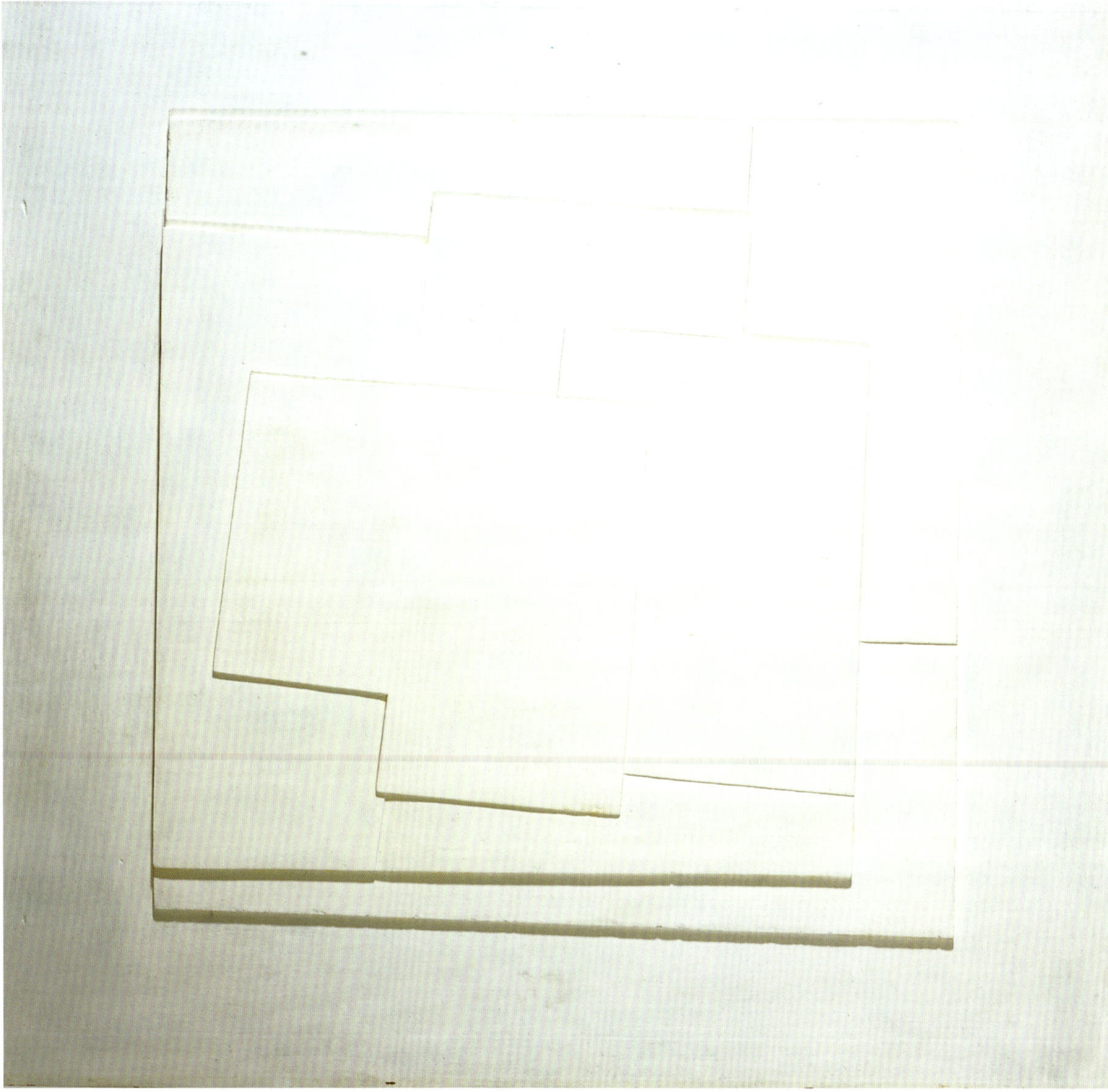

January 1962 (white relief, Paros)
62.2 x 63 cm (cat. 24)

rhythmical composition, playing off horizontals against arches and domes, taut lines of architecture and electricity wires against an undulating landscape background. Apart from the ironwork arabesques of the balcony and canopy, which, by being singled out, provide a comic note, all is pared down to essentials, yet evokes a strong sense of place.

Nicholson's intense concentration on his subject, while drawing it, fixed the details and the atmosphere deep in his memory. Later – and it could be years later – the memory might resurface from the subconscious while he was working on a relief and imbue it with the light, the texture or, more nebulously, the spirit of place. In this way it could be said that the drawings, or rather the particular experience of drawing, 'fed' the reliefs. But the connexions between the two, though strong, are not on the surface.

When Nicholson came to carve **White relief, Paros** (cat. 24) in January 1962, he had visited the island twice and made at least half a dozen drawings there. On returning from his first visit in 1959, he had tried to capture some aspects of the experience in four carved reliefs, each of them notable for colour and texture. Now the densely overlapping facets, carved in shallow recession and coated in a uniform white, are made to suggest the glare of Aegean sunlight rebounding from tall, whitewashed walls. White functions descriptively, not symbolically as in the white reliefs of the 1930s, just as the irregular, trapezoid shapes, including, uppermost, one of Nicholson's favourite 'axe heads', are far removed from the strictly rectilinear composition of those earlier reliefs.

One new, and even practical, development of the carved relief which gripped Nicholson's imagination from the late 1950s was that of the relief-wall. He found much post-war architecture depressingly arid and lacking in the poetry of form which he felt should grow naturally out of a building's function and its setting. Ideally he envisaged a collaboration between himself and the architect whereby, as part of the overall design (not as a last-minute afterthought), a large-scale, free-standing relief-wall would be so positioned that its colour and texture and the strong horizontal or vertical thrust of its carved shapes would animate the soullessly functional form of the building. Unfortunately this ideal collaboration never materialized, while the more imaginative architects came to devise ways of integrating poetry with function in the design of their buildings. The only project for a relief-wall ever to be realized at full scale (4 x 15 metres) was shown at the third Documenta at Kassel in 1964, but it was made of non-durable concrete and demolished at the end of the exhibition. Fortunately there remain a good number of projects for these walls,

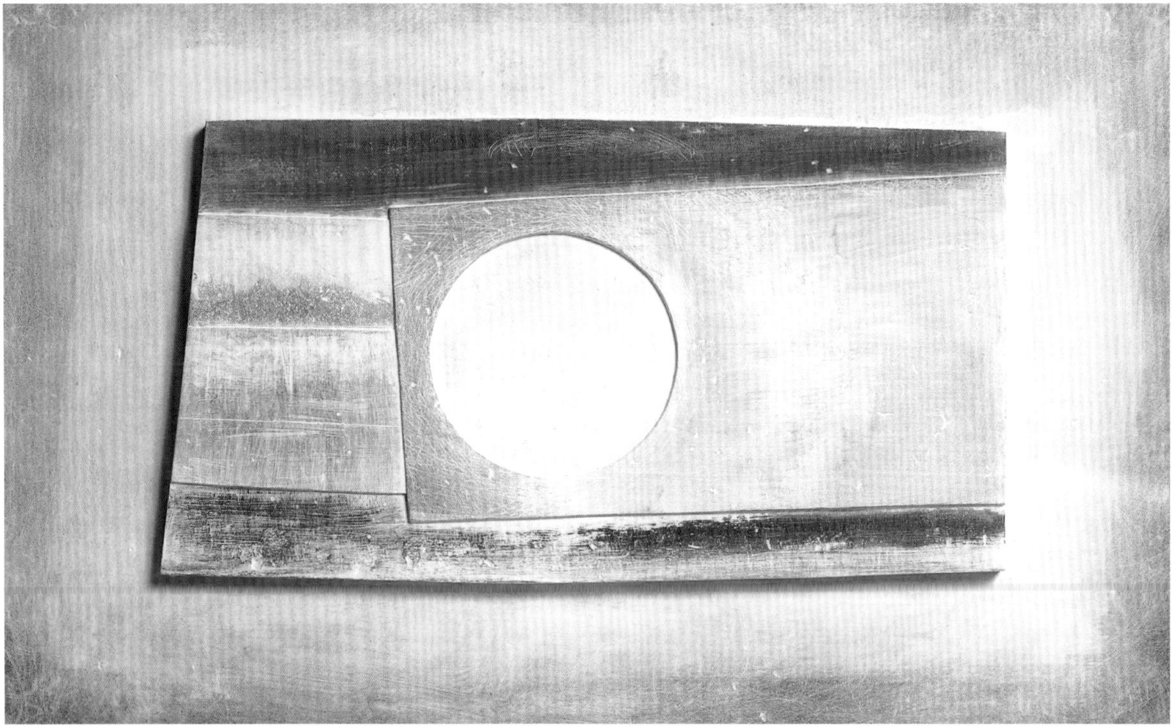

1965 (Kos - project for a free-standing relief-wall)
32 x 47 cm (cat. 30)

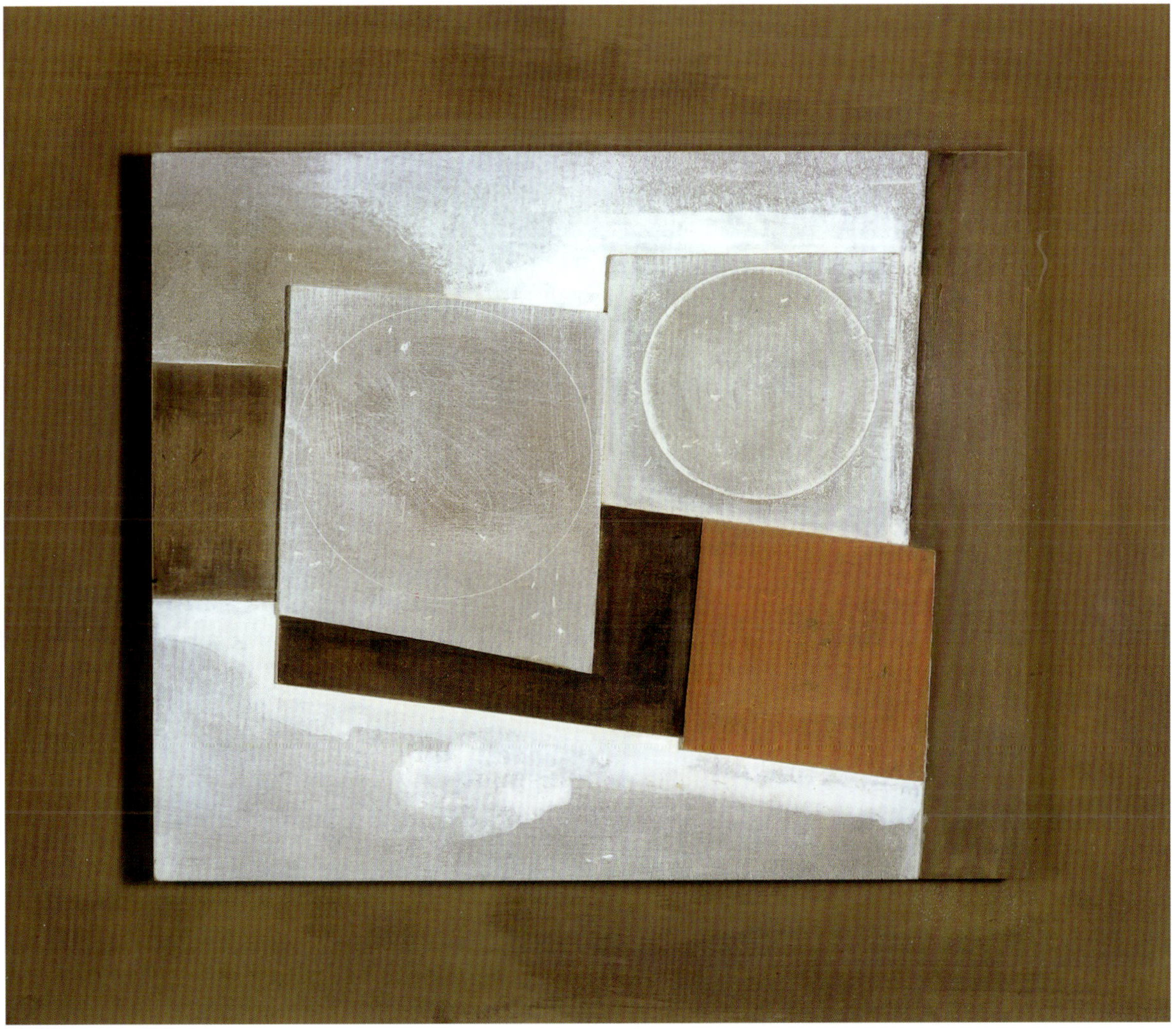

1968 (ramparts)
47.5 x 53.3 cm (cat. 35)

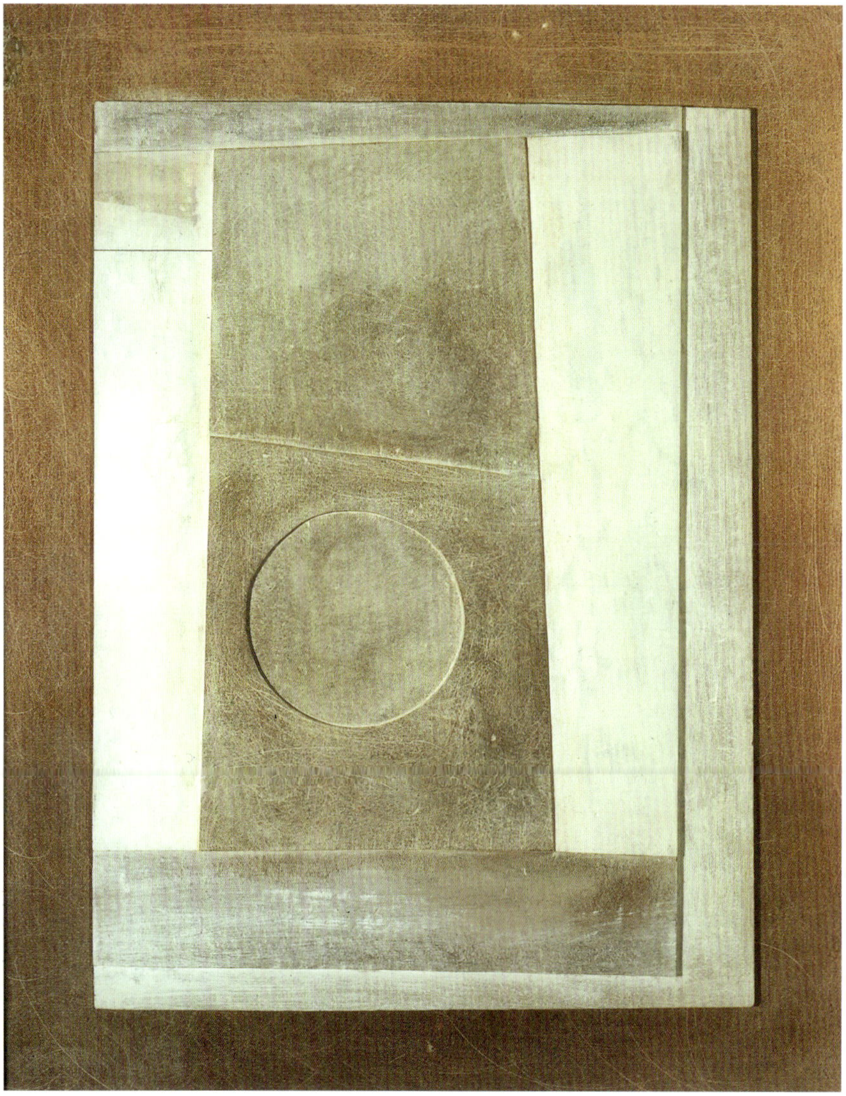

1966 (greystone)
56.5 x 47 cm (cat. 32)

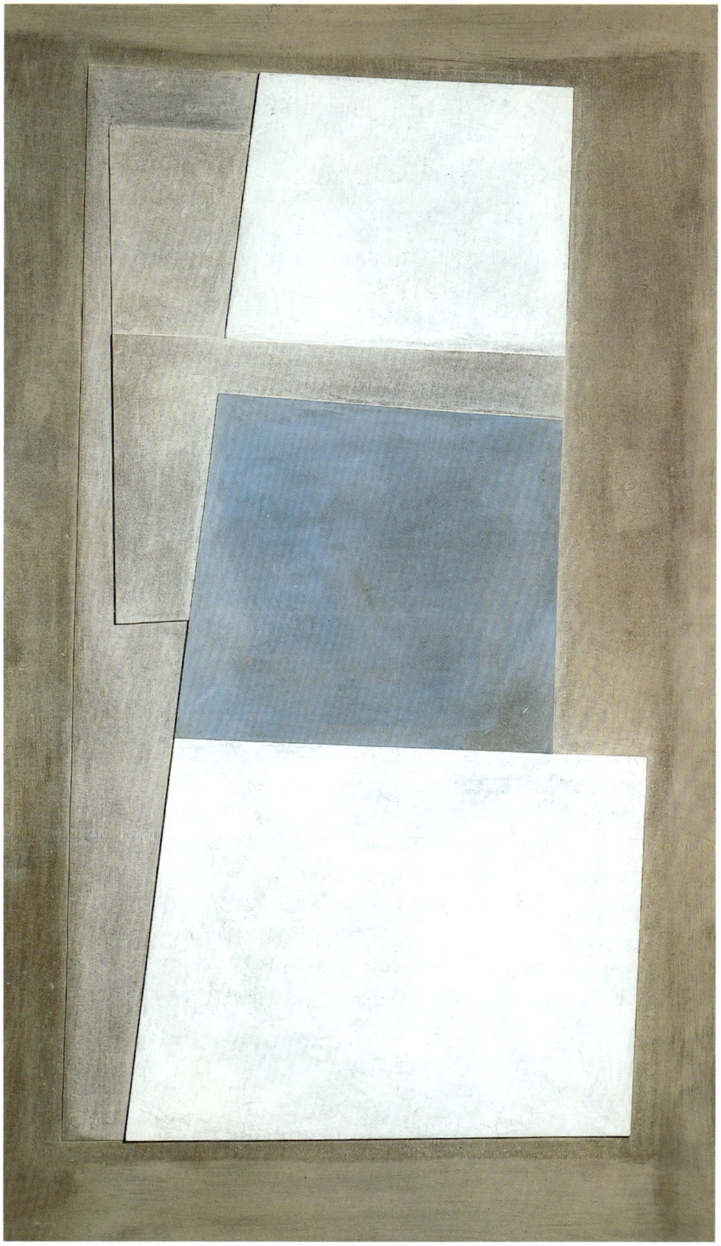

August 1964 (Racciano)
137.8 x 79.4 cm (cat. 29)

many of them quite small in size though monumental in scale and conception. By a paradox they are among Nicholson's most fully achieved works, lively, even dramatic, in composition, and with a superfine adjustment of texture, tone and colour to create luminosity and ever-changing spatial relations.

Many of Nicholson's late reliefs have place-names in their titles: Racciano, Kos, Obidos, Malta, Carnac, Aegina, Amboise. Sometimes the allusion is obvious, as in **White relief, Paros**, but more often it is not. He added these name-tags only after completing each work and the connexion between the two, whether close or distant, was always highly personal, even at times frivolous. The reliefs are rarely straightforward evocations of place: they are not so much landscapes as mindscapes. Above all, they are objects whose colour, form and texture are to be appreciated for themselves and for what they suggest to each individual viewer. They are a means of conveying an experience or an awareness, not the representation of something. Obviously this requires a special sort of aesthetic contemplation in the spectator who, if properly attuned, will enter into Nicholson's idea and so share with him a highly-charged piece of living reality. Just as for Nicholson it was a question of finding and recognizing the right mood before he could start on a drawing, or of going deeper and deeper into his subconscious as he scraped and painted and rubbed and scoured the bone-hard hardboard of his late reliefs, so we who contemplate the finished work must do so with sympathetic sensitivity, opening up our own memory-store to meet it halfway.

Familiarity with the landscape around Siena, though possibly a bonus, is not a requirement for becoming involved with the monumental **1970 (Sienese landscape)** (cat. 40). The eye is soon travelling back and forth between the two unequal quadrilaterals, lingering perhaps to wonder how it is that the lower, brown one seems to lead off into the distance; then it escapes up to the whitey-grey window of light before curiosity drives it back to inspect the loosely brushed paintmarks, bottom right, which contrast so shockingly with the superbly sweeping, shallow arcs, taut as the lines of a Nicholson drawing, that hold the work in dynamic suspension.

So much for what the eye may be doing, while incidentally registering the many subtle shifts of tone within the narrow colour range, the abrasions, the pockmarks and the strong contrast between the carved area and the backboard. While all this is happening you either are or are not making connexions between what you are seeing and what you have seen and experienced in the

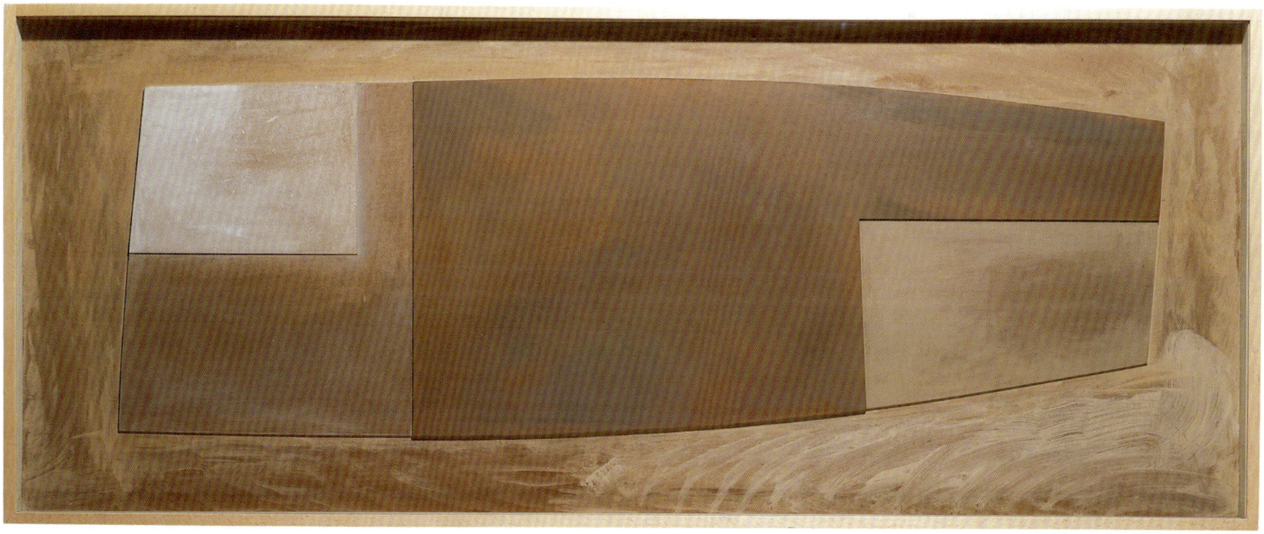

past. It may have nothing to do with Siena, or even with landscape. It may only be a feeling, a mood, a state of being. But the combined visual and affective experience can be powerful and enduring – as right for the viewer as it must have been for Nicholson the maker – quietening the mind, energizing the spirit.

1971-5 – full circle

After thirteen years in Switzerland Nicholson decided to return to England. The climate and landscape of the Ticino were ultimately not enough to counteract his growing feeling of isolation and the prospect of a lonely old-age. He came back alone: he and Felicitas had led increasingly independent lives and separation was accepted by both as inevitable (divorce following in 1977).

His new home was at Great Shelford, outside Cambridge, where his old friends Leslie and Sadie Martin lived in the former mill. Nicholson moved into the recently converted grain-store, named it The Flying Fox after a weather-vane on a nearby rooftop, and took delight in his surroundings. Returning to England – to where he felt he belonged and to old friends and

1970 (Sienese landscape)
73 x 177 cm (cat. 40)

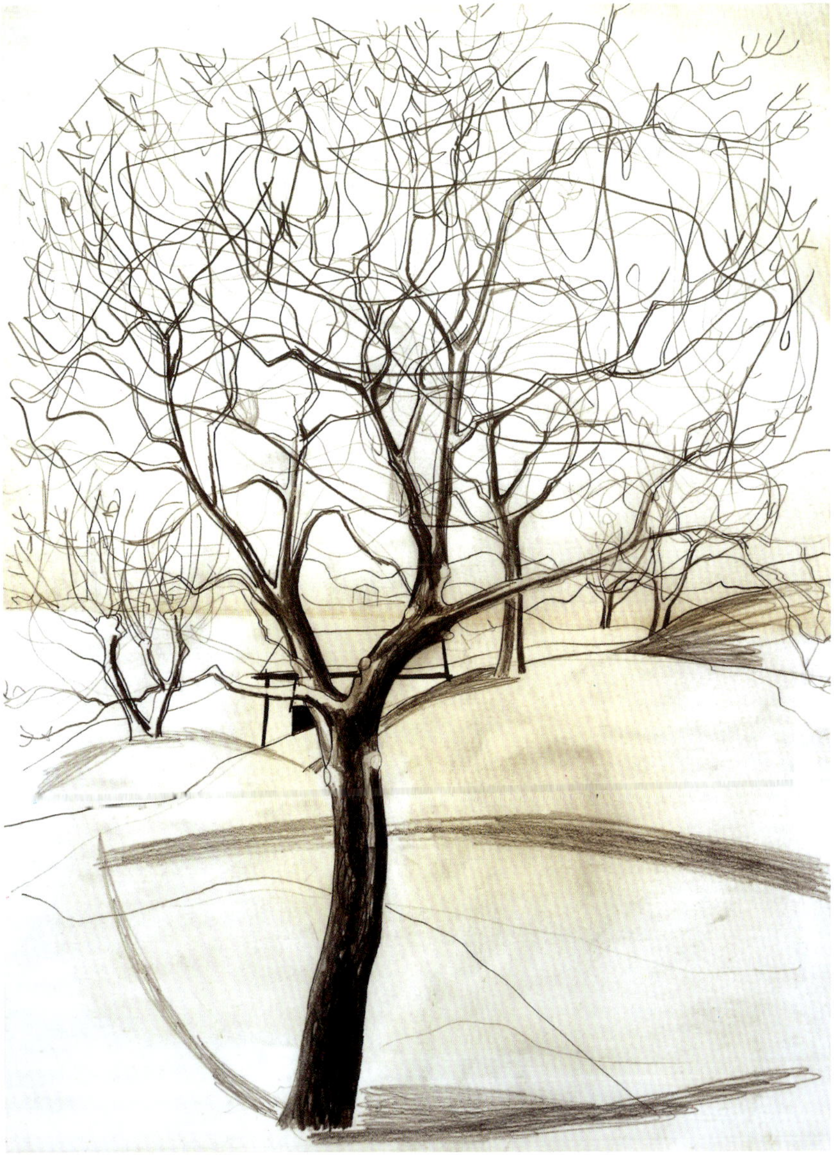

December 1958 (tree at Sava no.1)
51 x 35.5 cm (cat. 18)

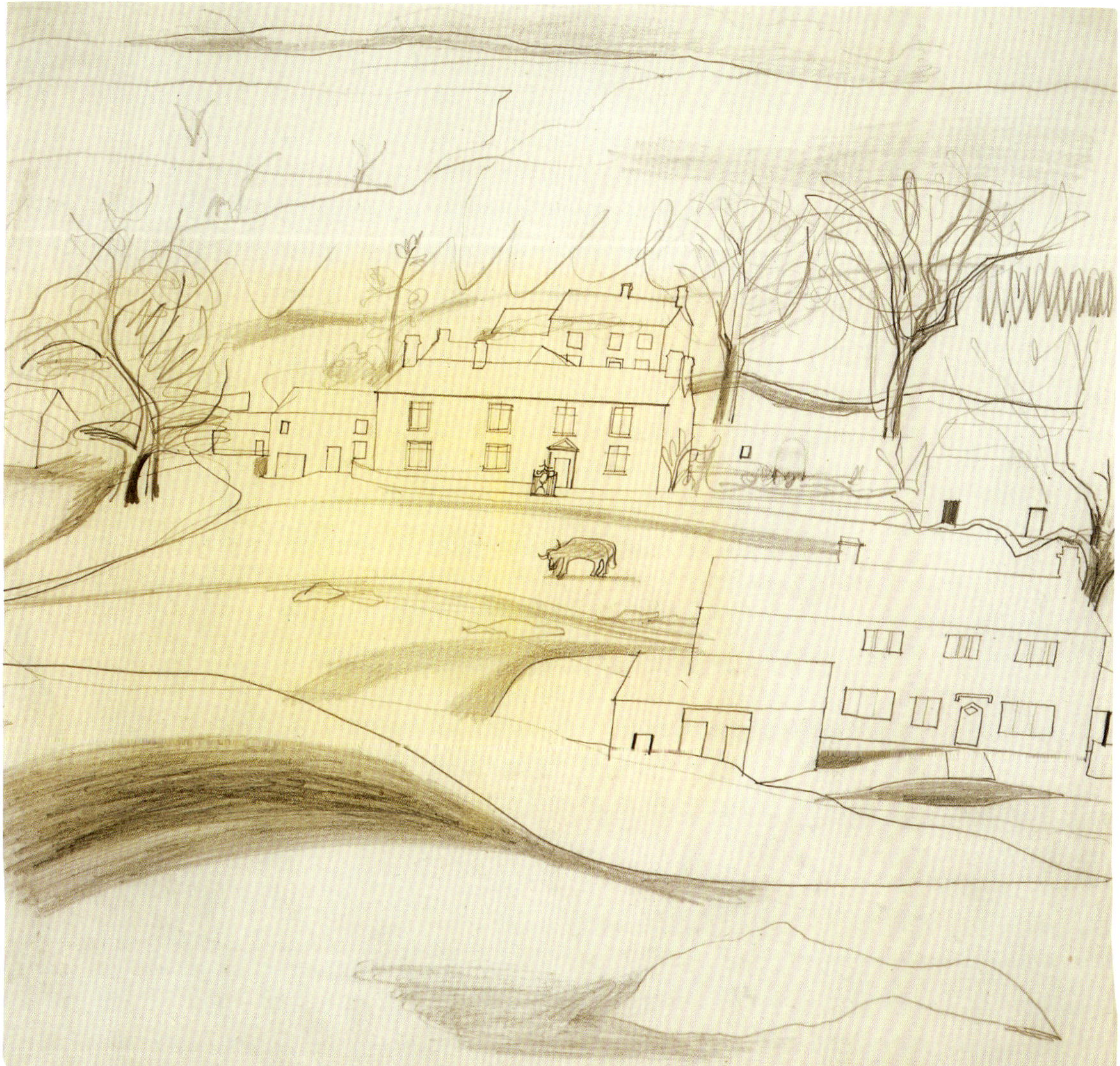

April 11 1954 (Yockenthwaite, Wharfedale)
39.5 x 38 cm (cat. 9)

associations – gave him a new zest, which was further increased by his meeting Angela Taunt at a party given by the Martins that Christmas of 1971. She already admired Nicholson's work and had herself taken up painting, while he was just then in need of the female support and enthusiasm always so essential to his well-being. It was an opportunity for both, and fortunately Angela was free to devote herself: her children were away at school and her husband, at that time over-occupied with university and college duties, gave generous encouragement. Nicholson, who had given up driving and now felt stranded, leapt at the offer of being driven. In May 1972 they went on the first of thirteen drawing trips they were to make together over the next six years, to Greece, Cyprus, Tuscany and Umbria as well as to various parts of England. This first expedition was, appropriately, to Yorkshire – to Wharfedale and around Rievaulx – Nicholson's favourite English landscape (apart from the Penwith peninsula) and over the years the inspiration for many fine drawings. One that he now made of the small church at **Hubberholme** (cat. 45) shows one aspect of his late drawing style, where the line is less taut, more relaxed, and the detail more whimsical than before. The cows ambling out to the left are not so different from the cat we met near the minaret of Kos, 'child's drawing', whether by Ben Nicholson or by David Hockney, being part of a general rejection of illusionism. The tree on the left of the tower is a close cousin of the tree Nicholson drew at Sava, near Taranto in Apulia, in 1958. (In that intensely vital drawing (cat. 18) note also the consciously non-illusionistic, 'babyish' shading.) A drawing made a couple of miles upstream from Hubberholme at **Yockenthwaite** in 1954 (cat. 9) is even more obviously in Nicholson's faux-naif style, harking back to his paintings of Cumbrian farmhouses in 1928-30, but also harking forward to the deliberately joky **May 1974 (Siena)** (cat. 52).

Comparing this, a little unfairly, with **May 1957 (Siena campanile)** (cat. 15), one of Nicholson's most arresting architectural drawings, the gentler touch, the more relaxed attitude and the tendency towards caricature in the later version are obvious, as is the similar playing off of empty space against intense and minute detail. The irregular shape of the paper in **May 1974 (Siena)** and the relation of the drawing to it make a telling contrast with the rigidly rectilinear version of 1957. But lest one should be tempted to dismiss the later Siena as simply the product of failing powers (and Nicholson *was* eighty when he drew it), one has only to compare **May 1974 (Certaldo)** (cat. 53), made in the same month, where the springing line seems effortlessly to create a complex architectural space, or **October 1972 (Gythian theatre)** (cat. 48), where the pencil marks are so fine as to seem etched into the paper.

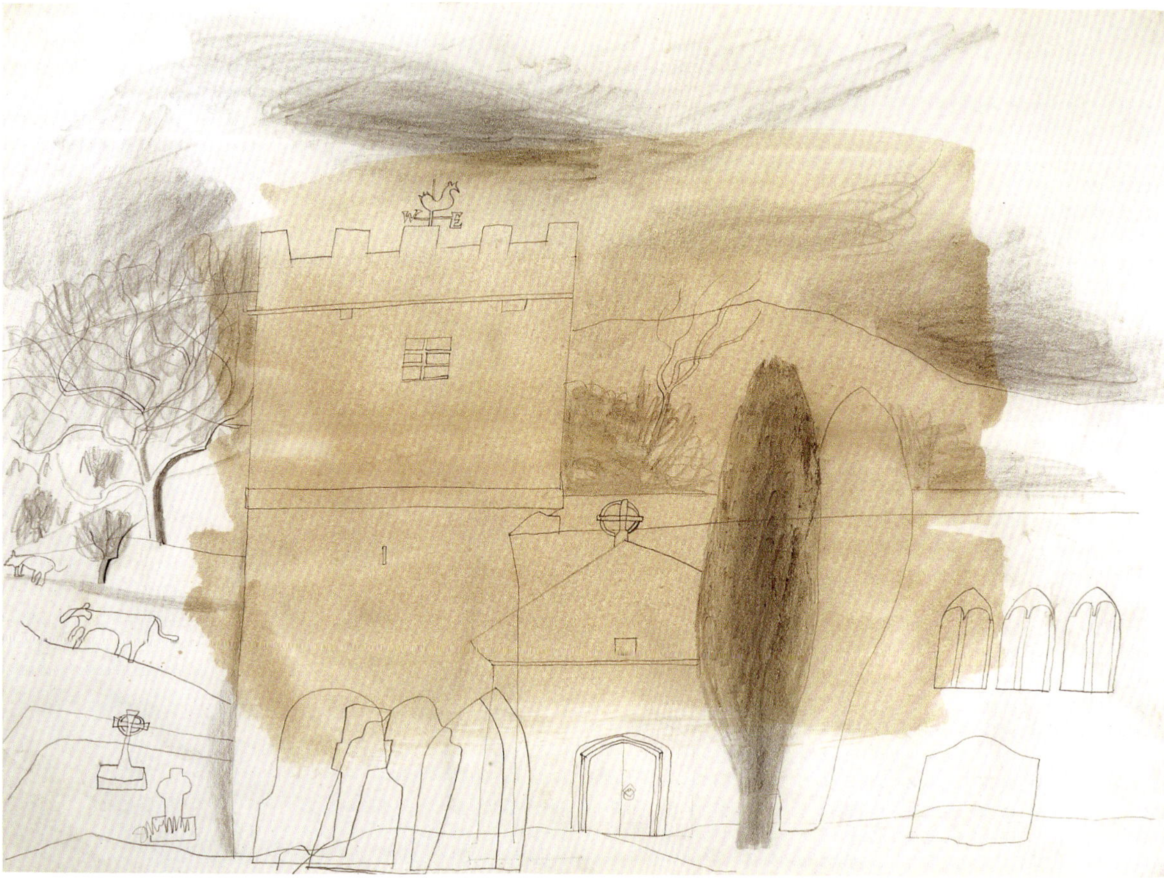

May 1972 (Hubberholme)
38 x 51 cm (cat. 45)

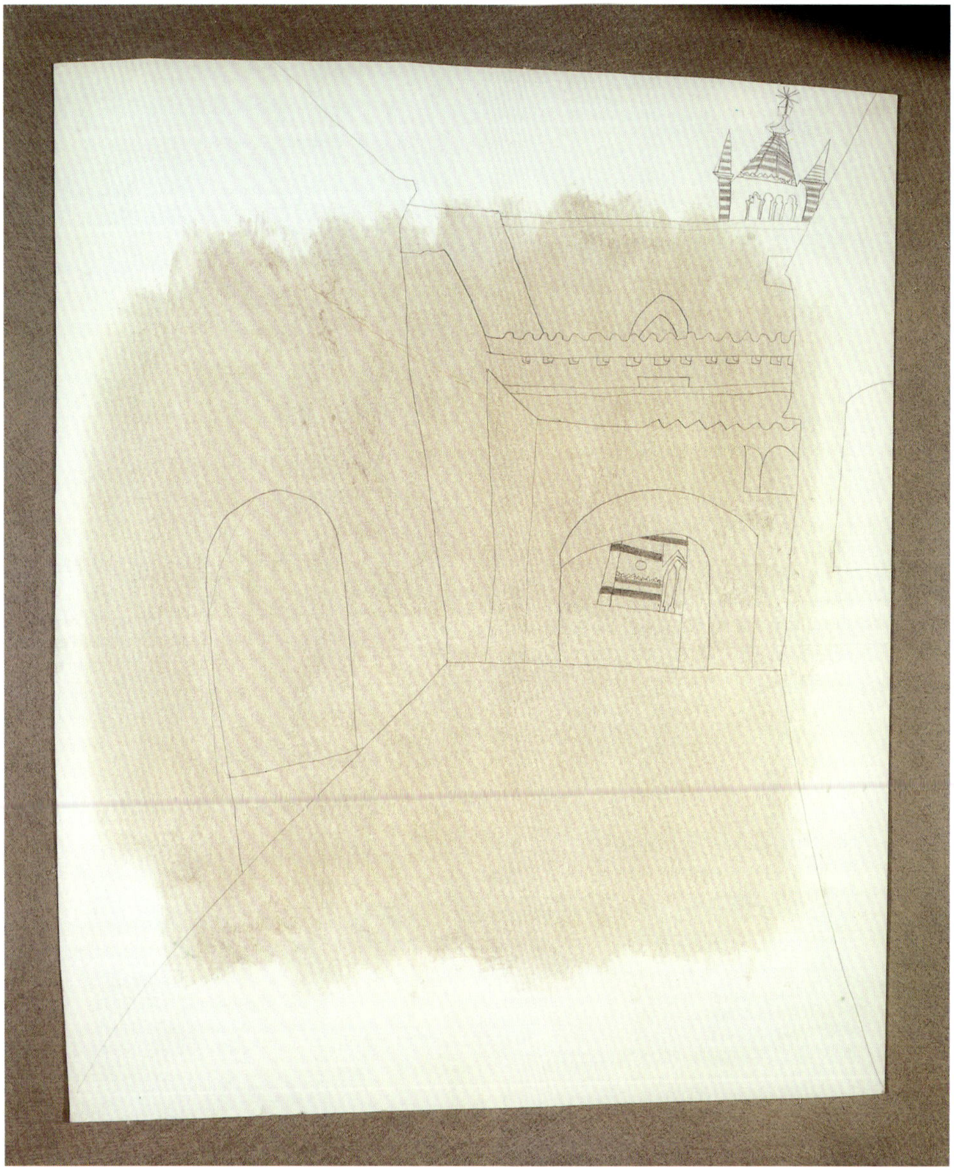

May 1974 (Siena)
59 x 49 cm (cat. 52)

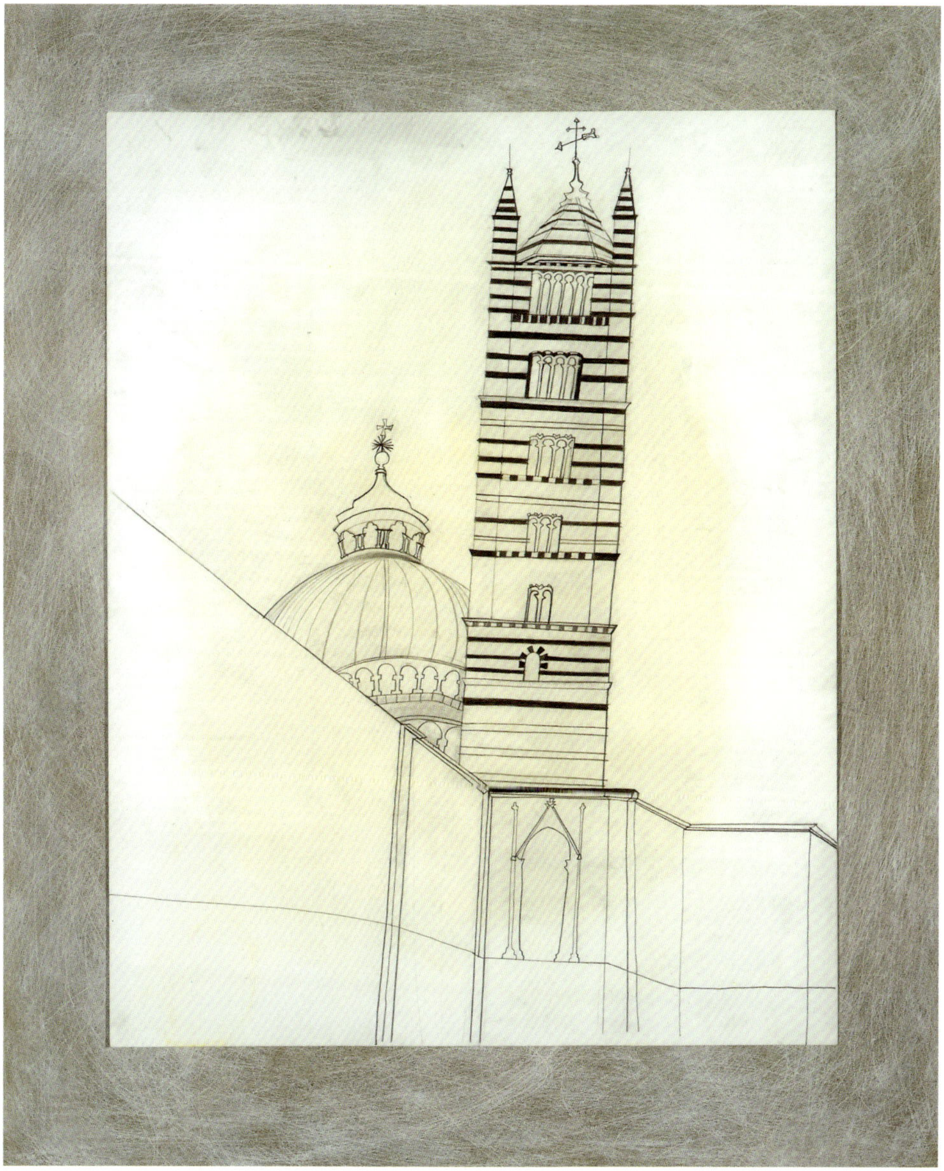

May 1957 (Siena campanile)
48 x 37 cm (cat. 15)

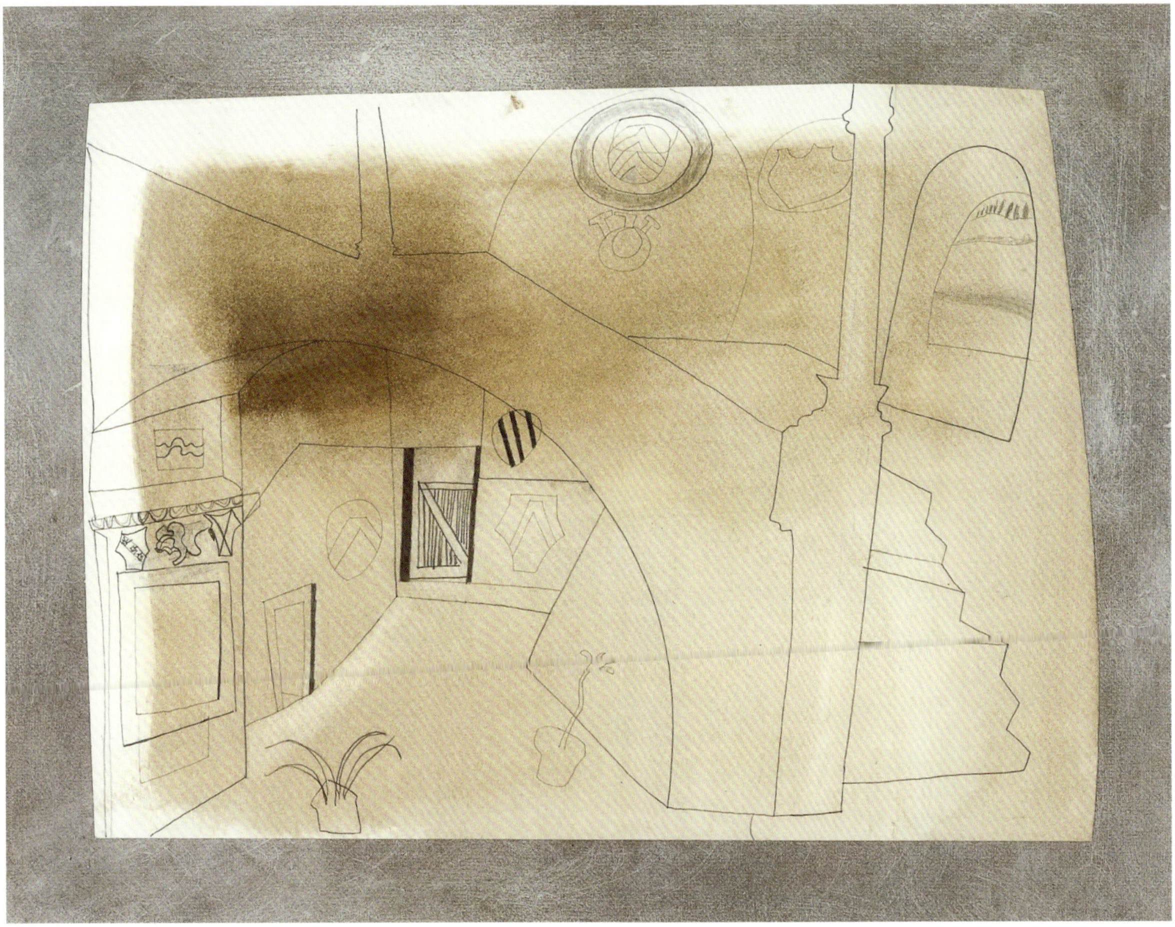

May 1974 (Certaldo)
54 x 68.5 cm (cat. 53)

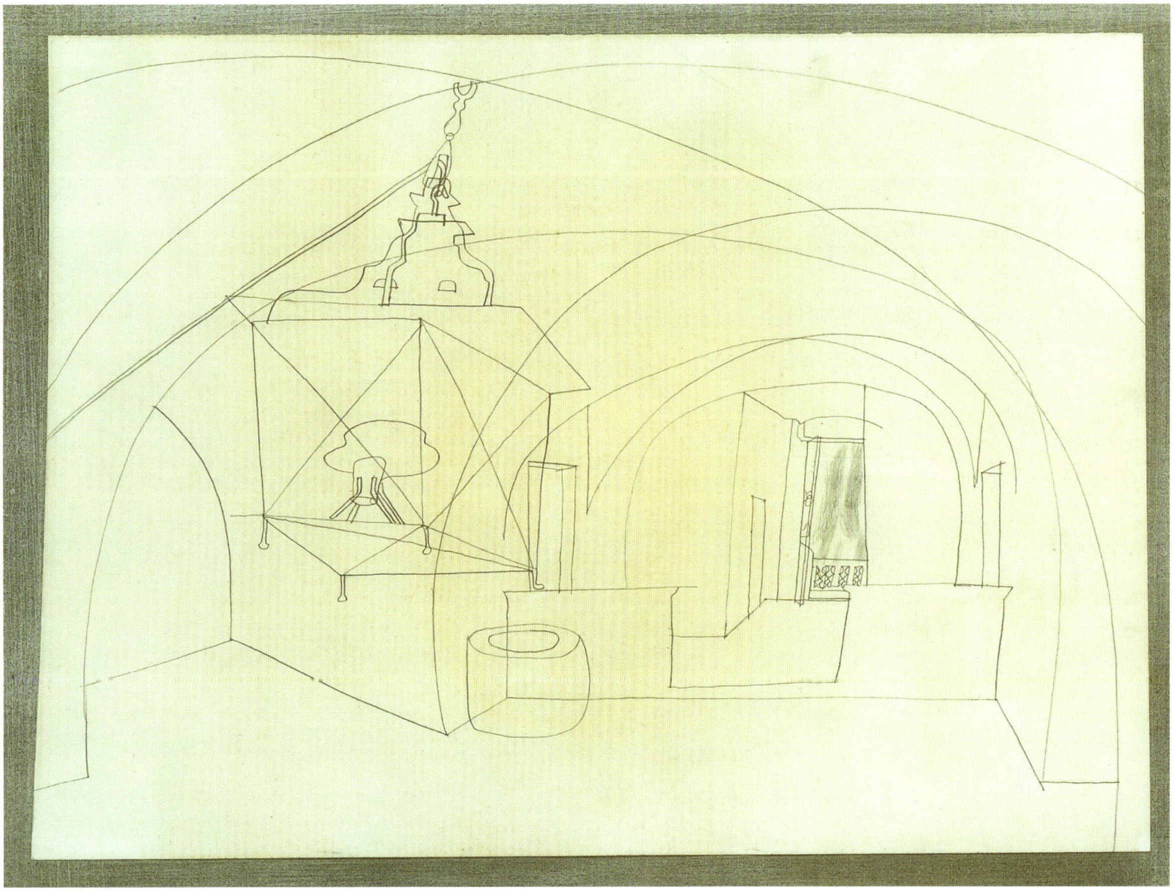

June 1962 (Palladio)
48.5 x 60 cm (cat. 25)

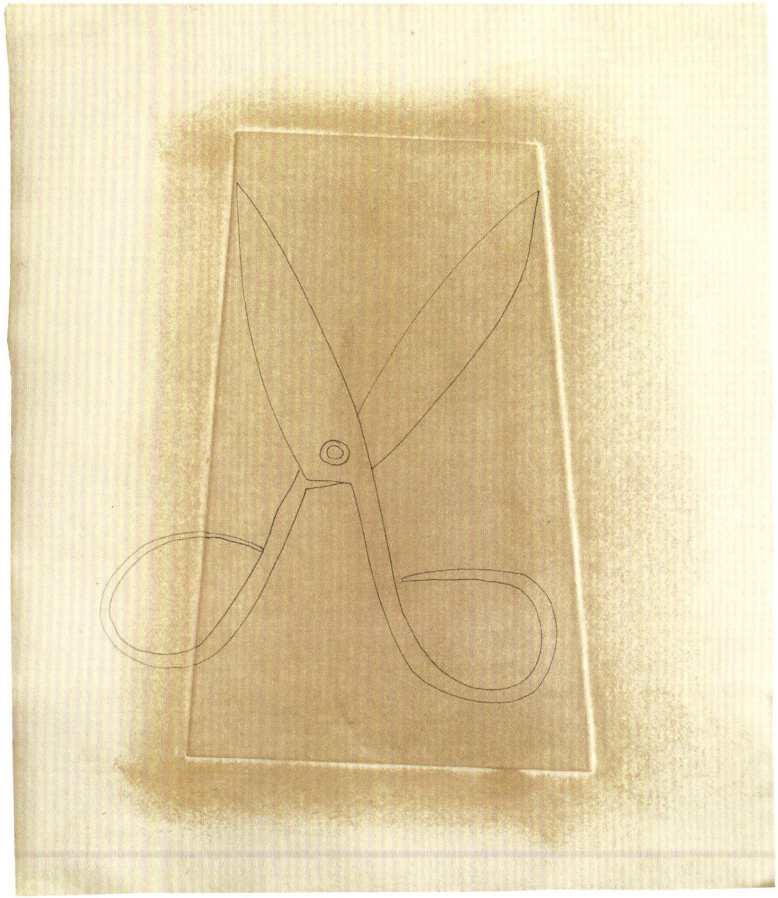

1968 (scissors, variation no.2)

38 x 32 cm (cat. 37)

A pair of hand-forged scissors, brought back from Greece by his daughter Kate, were the inspiration for a series of drawings in which Nicholson played ever more inventive variations on a theme. They were made at the time when he was producing etchings, and were drawn on the back of discarded pulls: the extra dimension made for greater immediacy. Now the starting-off point was not only the colour wash but also the impress of the etching plate, itself appearing in a variety of irregular shapes. Already in the early and uncomplicated second variation the life of the work hinges on the relation of the seemingly animate shears and handles to the geometric bounds of the relief.

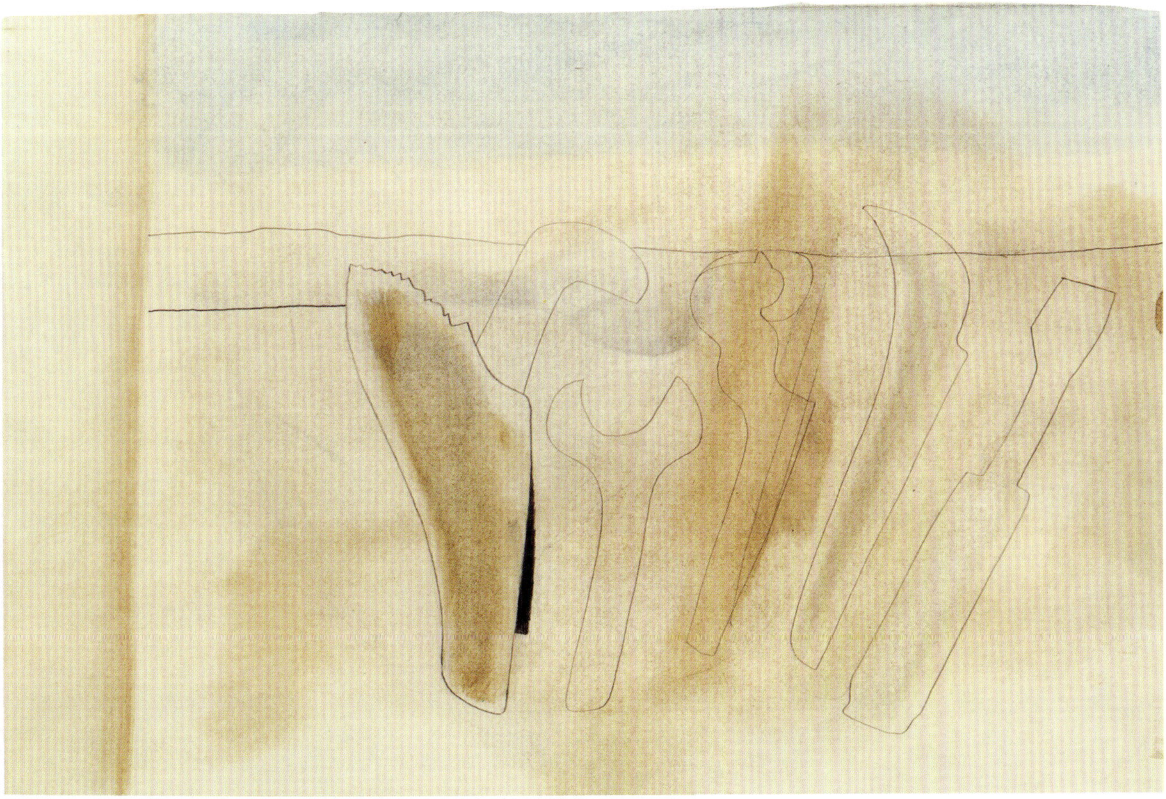

1973 (spanners, Holkham Sands 6)
34 x 50.5 cm (cat. 50)

Nothing better demonstrates Nicholson's continuing vitality and creativity than the series of almost forty oil-wash drawings he made in 1973-4, based on a set of plumber's tools (which he bought from a visiting plumber in exchange for a new set). No two of these variations are alike and in some the spanners and wrenches inhabit a world of poetic fantasy: in **1973 (spanners Holkham sands 6)** (cat. 50) they appear to be dancing the Lobster Quadrille on the Norfolk seashore.

It is not surprising that Nicholson in Cambridge came to feel like a fish out of water. And so in 1974 he moved to Hampstead, which he thought of as his home town: his small house in Pilgrim's Lane was more or less opposite where he had lived as a boy seventy years earlier. The studio space at The Flying Fox had been too small for him to carve reliefs, but now, after a gap of three years, he was able to resume. Before leaving Switzerland he had drawn up designs for the basic shapes of new reliefs which he intended to work on once back in England. A carpenter-friend had cut out the shapes and stuck them down onto backboards. Now, a little later than expected, Nicholson set about bringing these embryonic reliefs to life by scraping them with razor blades, scrubbing, scratching, cutting, rubbing (or occasionally brushing) paint on and off, and recutting. He felt that in these reliefs he had gone deeper than ever before into his sense of things, and some of them do indeed have a numinous quality. The veils of colour and light in **1974 (moonrise)** (cat. 51) suggest an infinity of space, leading one on to a contemplation of the void, as in some Far-Eastern painting. But this was the product of instinct and intuition – an idea gradually elicited after long hours of absolute concentration while working the material – not a conscious attempt to portray a reality underlying appearances. 'One just goes on chasing out something *alive*', as he once explained in a letter to Herbert Read (21 Aug 1944).

The fourteen reliefs exhibited at the Waddington Galleries in May 1976, most of them completed in the previous two years, were virtually the last Nicholson made. At the age of eighty-two he no longer had the strength to battle for hours with extremely resistant hardboard. Although Nicholson was still to produce a large number of mainly small-scale pen and oil-wash drawings, distinctively different from anything he had done before, thus proving himself full of invention to within months of his death in February 1982, this exhibition ends with his last pencil drawings and painted reliefs.

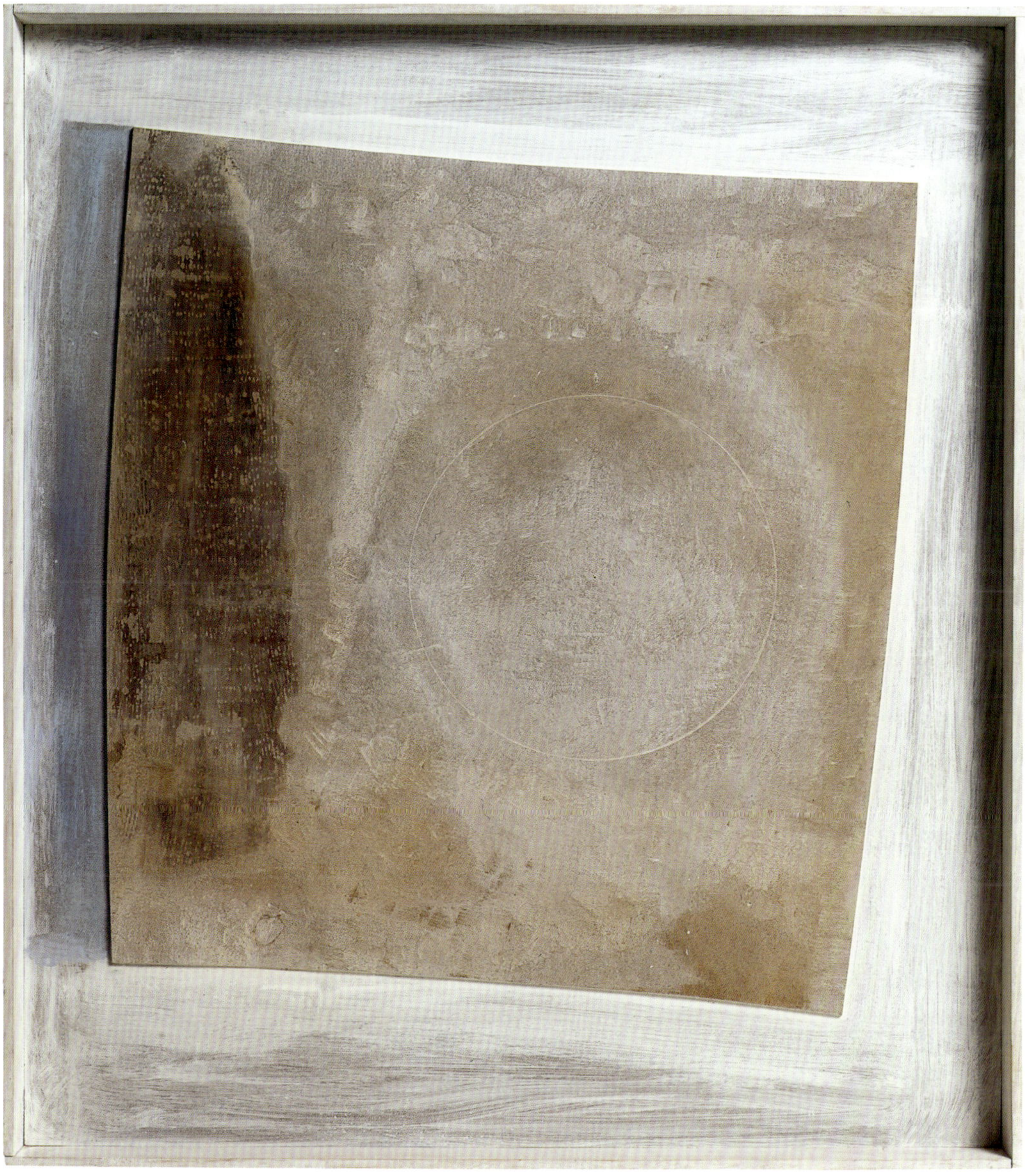

1974 (moonrise)
72 x 62 cm (cat. 51)

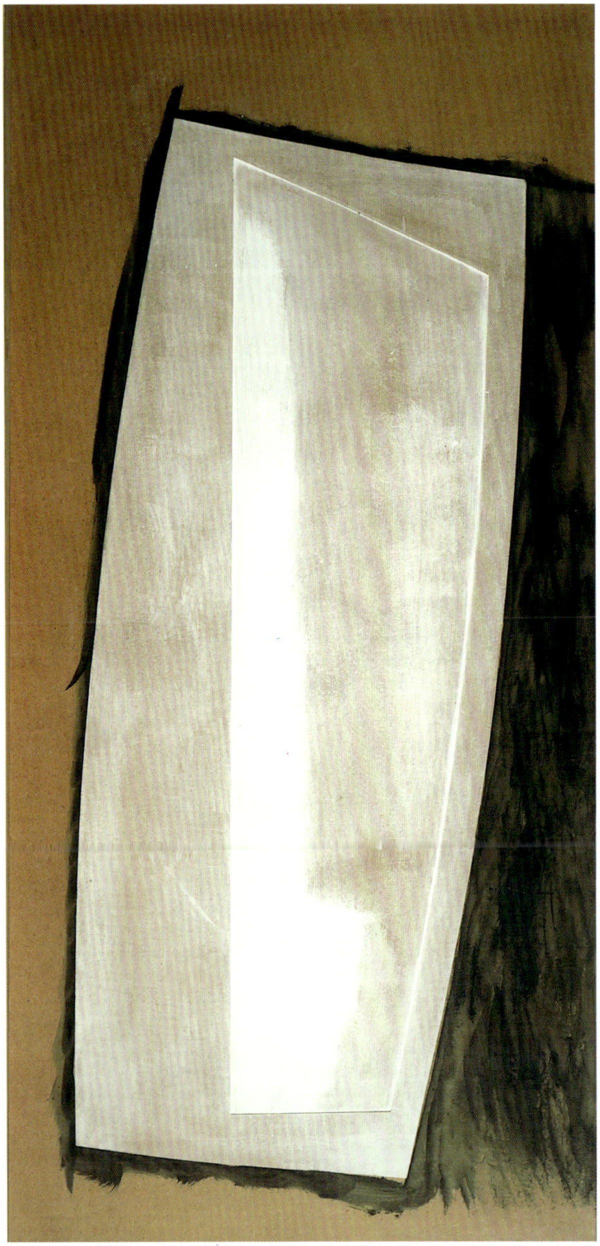

right

1971 (Obidos 2)
158 x 141.7 cm (cat. 43)

How much is this a memory-trace of the sunlit, whitewashed houses within the walled city of Obidos in Portugal, which Nicholson had visited in 1964? The answer, like the question, is beside the point. But we may think of the two excavated quadrilaterals, if only metaphorically, as blank windows – the tension between the upper and the lower echoing the grander tension between the near-rectangle that encloses them both and the near-square base behind it.

The curved shapes straining against each other provide the dynamic of the work, while the paint rubbed on and off its surface seems to defuse the tension with blurred edges and shifting depths. Nicholson's free handling of paint, here and in **1971 (dolphin)** (cat. 42), makes an exciting contrast with the precision of his carving and is particularly effective on this large scale.

left

1971 (dolphin)
167 x 68 cm (cat. 42)

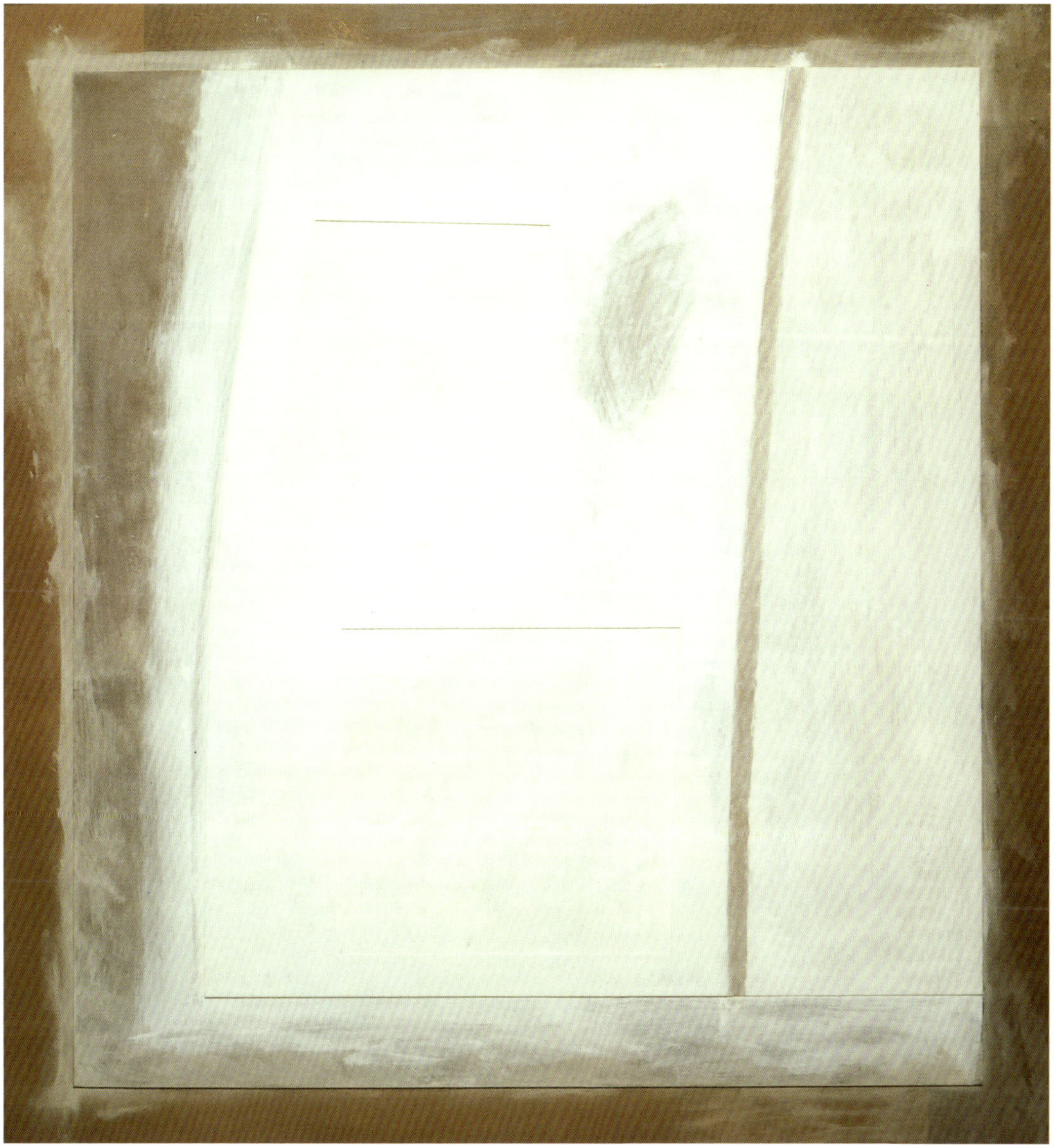

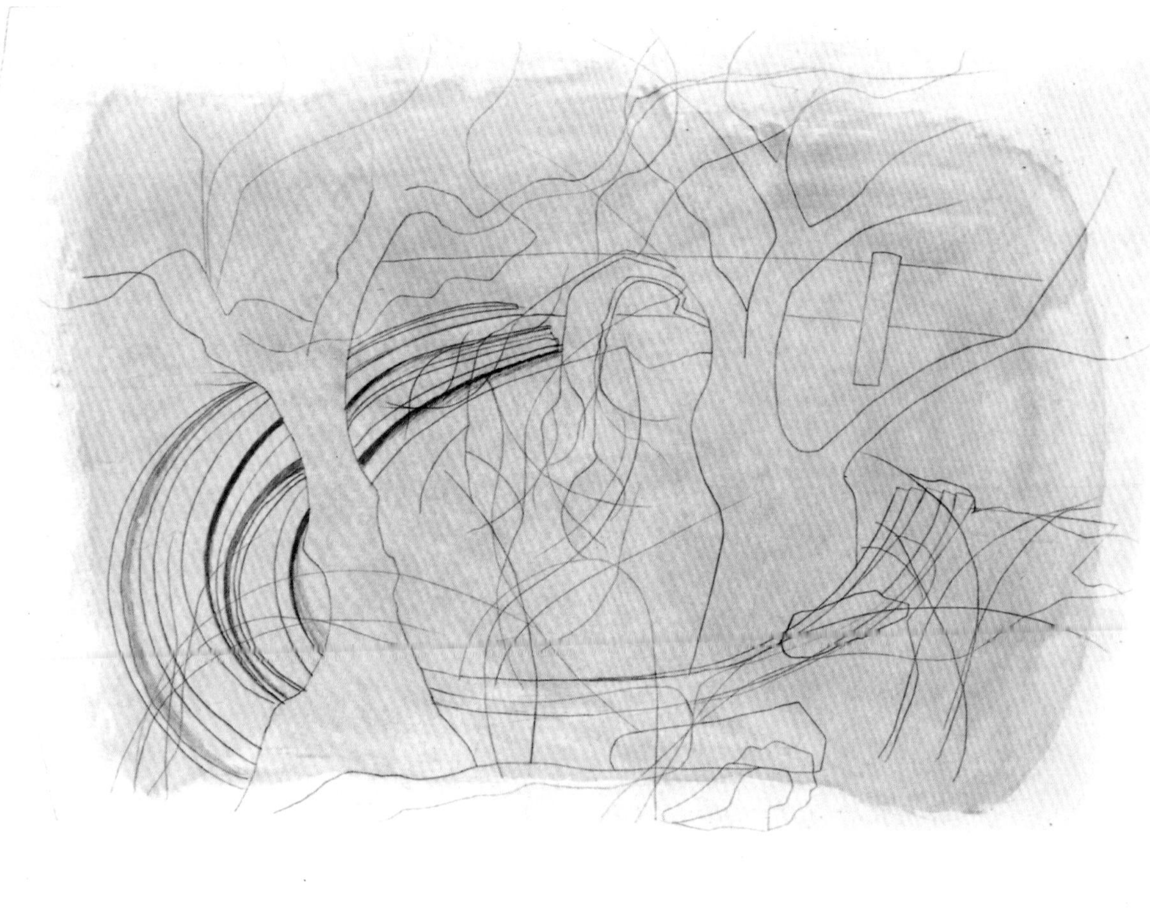

October 1972 (Gythian theatre)
53.2 x 67.3 cm (cat. 48)

CATALOGUE

1. **April 11 1950 (Newlyn)**
oil wash and pencil on paper, 35.5 x 51 cm
Trustees of the British Museum
(illustrated page 8)

2. **May 21 1950 (San Gimignano)**
pencil on paper, 35.5 x 51 cm
Private collection
(illustrated 10)

3. **May 22 1950 (cloisters, San Gimignano)**
oil wash and pencil on paper, 38.1 x 50.8 cm
Arts Council Collection, Hayward Gallery, London
(Southampton only)
(illustrated 11)

4. **May 22 1950 (La Buca, Tuscany)**
pencil on paper, 35.5 x 51 cm
Dr and Mrs W.T. Mason
(illustrated 10)

5. **May 24 1950 (single tower, San Gimignano)**
pencil on paper, 39 x 58 cm
Private collection
(illustrated 9)

6. **October 1951 (still life, steeple & ship)**
oil and pencil on board, 20 x 35.5 cm
Private collection, England
(Cambridge and Manchester only)
(illustrated 13)

7. **January 4 1953 (Thorpe, Wharfedale in snow)**
oil wash and pencil on paper, 38 x 56 cm
Pallant House Gallery, Chichester.
Hussey Bequest, 1985
(Cambridge and Manchester only)

8. **March 26 1954 (bird and spots)**
oil wash and pencil on paper, 40.5 x 53.3 cm
Trustees of the Cecil Higgins Art Gallery, Bedford

9. **April 11 1954 (Yockenthwaite, Wharfedale)**
oil wash and pencil on paper, 39.5 x 38 cm
Deutsche Bank Collection, London
(illustrated 41)

10. **May 12 1954 (portrait of the artist)**
oil wash and pencil on paper, 29 x 34 cm
Private collection
(illustrated 12)

11. **August 13 1954 (St Agnes, Cornwall)**
oil wash and pencil on paper, 39 x 56.5 cm
Ivor Braka Ltd., London

12. **October 2 1955 (metallic landscape, Buonconvento)**
oil wash and pencil on paper, 36 x 43.9 cm
The Ashmolean Museum, Oxford.
Bequeathed by Mrs M. Broke Freeman
(Cambridge and Manchester only)
(illustrated 15)

13. **October 5 1955 (cathedral, Pienza)**
oil wash and pencil on paper, 53 x 40.7 cm
Trustees of the Cecil Higgins Art Gallery, Bedford
(illustrated 14)

14. **May 22 1956 (hendrifter)**
oil on carved board, 36 x 43 cm
Arts Council Collection, Hayward Gallery, London
(illustrated 27)

15. **May 1957 (Siena campanile)**
oil wash and pencil on paper, 48 x 37 cm
Private collection
(illustrated 45)

16. **1957 (Rievaulx Abbey)**
oil wash and pencil on paper, 35.5 x 48.2 cm
Bernard Jacobson Gallery
(illustrated 17)

17. **April 1958 (Prato)**
oil wash and pencil on paper, 34 x 29.5 cm
Private collection
(illustrated 19)

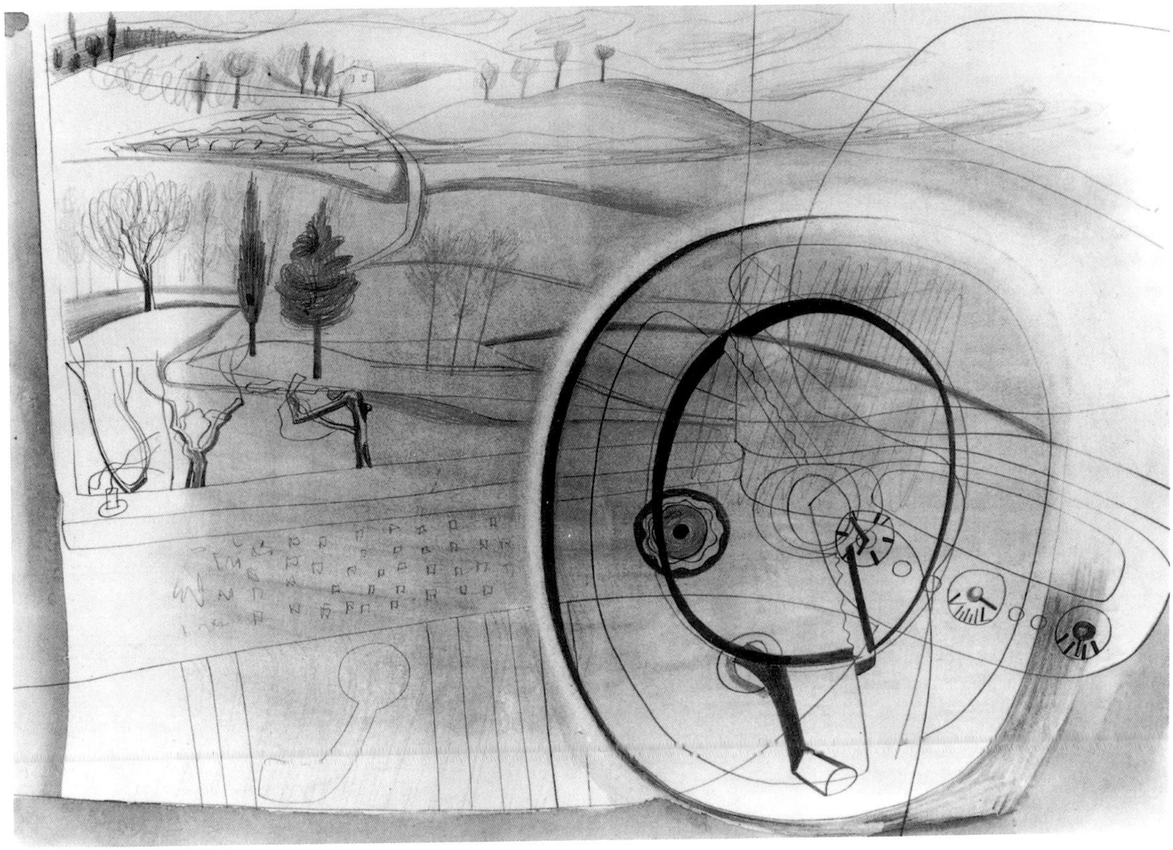

April 1959 (Racciano from car)

oil wash and pencil on paper, 43.5 x 56.5 cm *(not exhibited)*

Rain or cold were the occasion for Nicholson to make drawings from the shelter of his car. The landscape is framed by the windscreen or, as here, by the side-window, and offset by the lovingly depicted detail of dashboard and steering-wheel in the foreground. Once again the manmade and mechanical are contrasted with the natural world.

18. **December 1958 (tree at Sava no.1)**
oil wash and pencil on paper, 51 x 35.5 cm
Kirklees Metropolitan Council, Huddersfield Art Gallery
(illustrated 40 and back cover)

19. **April 1959 (Racciano swift)**
oil wash and pencil on paper, 49.8 x 63.5 cm
Private collection

20. **April 1959 (Kos)**
oil wash and pencil on cardboard, 48 x 35.2 cm
Private collection
(illustrated 30)

21. **June 1961 (Alnwick)**
oil and pencil on board, 80 x 82.5 cm
David Thomson
(illustrated 21)

22. **June 1961 (goblet and blue square)**
oil and pencil on board, 80 x 80 cm
Scottish National Gallery of Modern Art, Edinburgh
(Cambridge and Manchester only)
(illustrated 20)

23. **September 1961 (Paros chapel)**
oil wash and pencil on paper, 40 x 49.5 cm
Tate. Purchased 1968
(illustrated 31)

24. **January 1962 (white relief, Paros)**
oil on carved board, 62.2 x 63 cm
Scottish National Gallery of Modern Art, Edinburgh
(illustrated 32)

25. **June 1962 (Palladio)**
oil wash and pencil on paper, 48.5 x 60 cm
Private collection
(illustrated 47)

26. **July 1962 (white jug)**
pencil on paper, 49.5 x 61.5 cm
Private collection
(illustrated 23)

27. **October 1962 (three circles)**
oil wash and pencil on board, 35.6 x 33 cm
Tate. Presented by the artist 1968
(illustrated 23)

28. **1964 (Patmos - project for a free-standing relief-wall)**
oil on carved board, 41 x 62.5 cm
Private collection, Switzerland

29. **August 1964 (Racciano)**
oil on carved board, 137.8 x 79.4 cm
The British Council Collection
(illustrated 37)

30. **1965 (Kos - project for a free-standing relief-wall)**
oil on carved board, 32 x 47 cm
Private collection
(illustrated 34)

31. **1966 (Saronikos)**
oil on carved board, 74 x 128 cm
Helly Nahmad Gallery, London
(illustrated 29)

32. **1966 (greystone)**
oil and pencil on carved board, 56.5 x 47 cm
Southampton City Art Gallery
(illustrated 36)

33. **1966 (vertical wall)**
oil on carved board, 43.2 x 26.7 cm
Tate. Presented by the artist 1979
(illustrated 28)

34. **1967 (nest of circles)**
oil on carved board, 147.3 x 71.1 cm
Tate. Presented by the artist 1968

35. **1968 (ramparts)**
oil on carved board, 47.5 x 53.3 cm
Private collection, London
(illustrated 35)

36. **1968 (green still life)**
oil wash and pencil on paper, 49 x 41 cm
Private collection
(illustrated 16)

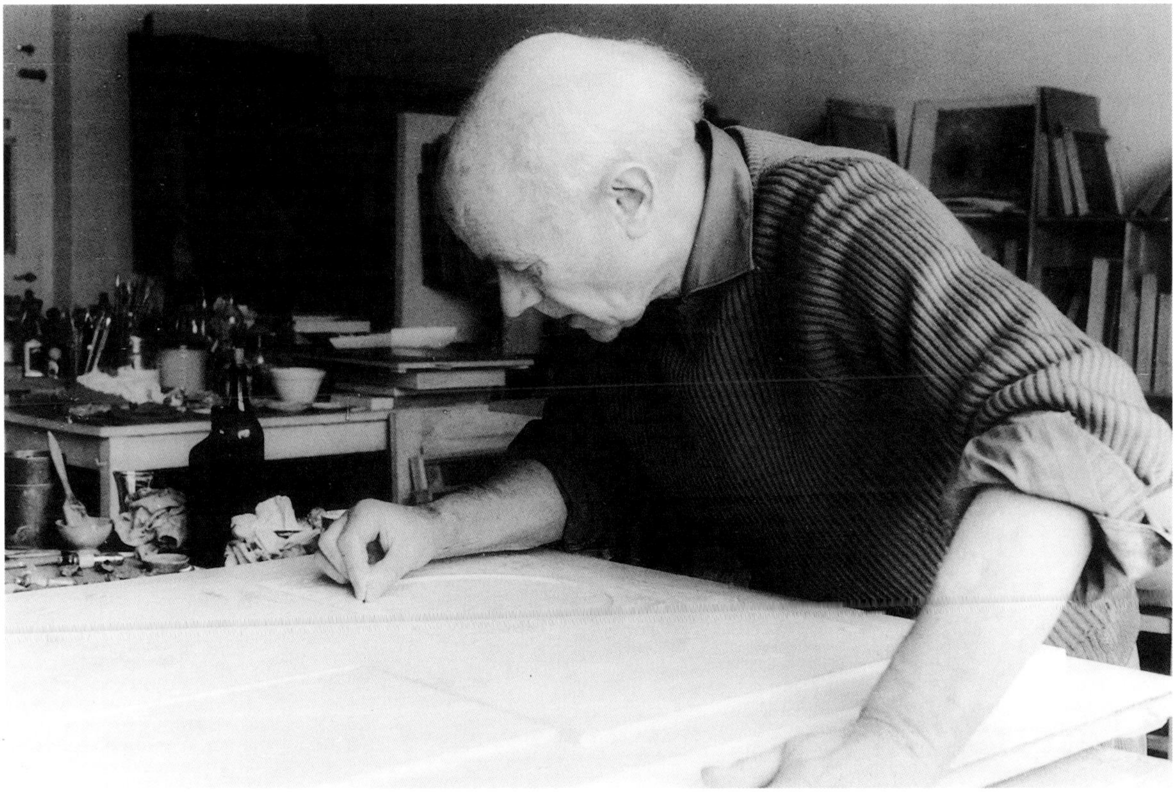

Ben Nicholson in his studio at Casa alla Rocca

37. **1968 (scissors, variation no.2)**
relief drawing, oil wash and pencil on paper impressed by etching plate, 38 x 32 cm
Private collection
(illustrated 48)

38. **1968 (crescent moonlight)**
oil and pencil on board, 56.5 x 50.8 cm
Private collection, Germany
(illustrated 1)

39. **1969 (Rievaulx no.1)**
oil wash and pencil on paper, 59 x 49 cm
Private collection

40. **1970 (Sienese landscape)**
oil on carved board, 73 x 177 cm
Private collection, London, courtesy Robert Sandelson Gallery
(illustrated 39)

41. **1970 (Lavenham)**
oil wash and pencil on paper, 62 x 50 cm
Private collection
(illustrated 25)

42. **1971 (dolphin)**
oil on carved board, 167 x 68 cm
Helly Nahmad Gallery, London
(illustrated 52 and front cover)

43. **1971 (Óbidos 2)**
oil on carved board, 158 x 141.7 cm
Helly Nahmad Gallery, London
(illustrated 53)

44. **1971 (Malta)**
oil on carved board, 51 x 107 cm
Dr and Mrs W T Mason

45. **May 1972 (Hubberholme)**
oil wash and pencil on paper, 38 x 51 cm
Private collection
(illustrated 43)

46. **August 1972 (still life with some blue)**
oil wash and pencil on paper, 38 x 35 cm
Diamond Trading Company Art Collection
(illustrated 24)

47. **October 1972 (Olympia)**
oil wash and pencil on paper, 44.6 x 66.5 cm
Private collection

48. **October 1972 (Gythian theatre)**
oil wash and pencil on paper, 53.2 x 67.3 cm
Rüdiger K. Weng, Viersen, Germany
(illustrated 54)

49. **1972 (three red stripes on blue)**
oil wash and pencil on paper, 40.7 x 31.2 cm
Private collection

50. **1973 (spanners, Holkham Sands 6)**
oil wash and pencil on paper, 34 x 50.5 cm
Private collection
(illustrated 49)

51. **1974 (moonrise)**
oil on carved board, 72 x 62 cm
Private collection
(illustrated 51)

52. **May 1974 (Siena)**
oil wash and pencil on paper, 59 x 49 cm
Private collection
(illustrated 44)

53. **May 1974 (Certaldo)**
oil wash, pencil and ink on paper, 54 x 68.5 cm
Private collection
(illustrated 46)

54. **May 1974 (Lucignano)**
oil wash and pencil on paper, 76.2 x 61.3 cm
Tate. Presented by the artist 1976

55. **1962-75 (wall project)**
oil on carved board, 27.3 x 61.3 cm
Tate. Presented by the artist 1979

56. **May 1976 (Muchelney Abbey with bird)**
oil wash and pencil on paper, 55 x 55 cm
Private Collection

KETTLE'S YARD

Kettle's Yard, University of Cambridge	27 July – 22 September 2002
Whitworth Art Gallery, University of Manchester	3 October – 15 December 2002
Southampton City Art Gallery	9 January – 16 March 2003

exhibition selected by Peter Khoroche

catalogue designed by Paul Allitt, printed by Hilo Colour Printers Ltd, Colchester

Photographs by Felicitas Vogler (pp. 4, 18, 58), Cyril Reddihough (p.12),

Photographs of works by James Austin, Prudence Cuming, Mike Fear, John Webb and Gareth Winters

ISBN 0 907074 95 2

This and other Kettle's Yard publications are available from

Kettle's Yard, Castle Street, Cambridge, CB3 0AQ

telephone 01223 352124 • www.kettlesyard.cam.ac.uk